TRICKSTER FEMINISM

BOOKS, CHAPBOOKS, AND COLLABORATIONS
BY ANNE WALDMAN

On the Wing

O My Life!

Giant Night

Baby Breakdown

Memorial Day (with Ted Berrigan)

No Hassles

The West Indies Poems

Life Notes: Selected Poems

Self Portrait (with Joe Brainard)

Sun the Blonde Out

Fast Speaking Woman

Journals & Dreams

Shaman/Shamane

Sphinxeries (with Denyse Du Roi)

Polar Ode (with Eileen Myles)

Countries (with Reed Bye)

Cabin

First Baby Poems

Makeup on Empty Space

Invention (with Susan Hall)

Den Mond in Farbe Sehen

Skin Meat Bones

The Romance Thing

Blue Mosque

Tell Me About It: Poems for Painters

Helping the Dreamer: New & Selected Poems, 1966–1988

Her Story (with Elizabeth Murray)

Not a Male Pseudonym

Lokapala

Fait Accompli

Troubairitz

Iovis: All Is Full of Jove

Kill or Cure

Iovis II

Kin (with Susan Rothenberg)

Polemics (with Anselm Hollo & Jack Collom)

Homage to Allen G. (with George Schneeman)

Donna Che Parla Veloce

Young Manhattan (with Bill Berkson)

One Voice in Four Parts (with Richard Tuttle)

Marriage: A Sentence

Au Lit/Holy (with Eleni Sikelianos & Laird Hunt)

Zombie Dawn (with Tom Clark)

Dark Arcana/Afterimage or Glow

In the Room of Never Grieve: New & Selected Poems, 1985–2003

Fleuve Flâneur (with Mary Kite & Dave Kite)

Structure of the World Compared to a Bubble

Outrider

Femme Qui Parle Vite

Red Noir

Nine Nights Meditation (with Donna Dennis)

Martyrdom

Manatee/Humanity

Matriot Acts

The Iovis Trilogy: Colors in the Mechanism of Concealment

Soldatesque/Soldiering (with Noah Saterstrom)

Cry Stall Gaze (with Pat Steir)

Gossamurmur

Archives, Pour Un Monde Menacé

Aubaderrying

Empty Set (with Alexis Myre)

Jaguar Harmonics

Sweet-Voiced [Mutilated] Papyrus (with Pamela Lawton)

Fantastic Caryatids (with Vincent Katz)

Extinction Aria

Voice's Daughter of a Heart Yet to Be Born

TRICKSTER FEMINISM

ANNE WALDMAN

PENGUIN POETS

PENGUIN BOOKS

An imprint of Penguin Random House LLC
375 Hudson Street
New York, New York 10014
penguinrandomhouse.com

Pages xiii, 139–141 constitute an extension of this copyright page.

LIBRARY OF CONGRESS CATALOGING-IN-PUBLICATION DATA
Names: Waldman, Anne, 1945– author.
Title: Trickster feminism / Anne Waldman.
Description: New York, New York : Penguin Books, [2018] |
Series: Penguin poets
Identifiers: LCCN 2017060641 (print) | LCCN 2018003371 (ebook) |
ISBN 9780525504344 (ebook) | ISBN 9780143132363 (softcover)
Subjects: | BISAC: POETRY / American / General. | SOCIAL SCIENCE / Feminism &
Feminist Theory.
Classification: LCC PS3573.A4215 (ebook) | LCC PS3573.A4215 A6 2018 (print) |
DDC 811/.54—dc23
LC record available at https://lccn.loc.gov/2017060641

Printed in the United States of America

3 5 7 9 10 8 6 4 2

Set in Fournier MT Std

Designed by Catherine Leonardo

in memoriam

~ Pauline Oliveros ~ Joanne Kyger ~ Geri Allen ~

pushing against the darkness many decades
with silence, poetry, sound, wit,
radical exploratory consciousness

"I am so happy in the silky damp dark of the labyrinth and there is no thread."

—Hélène Cixous

"I have important work for you to do . . . There are many bad creatures on earth. You will have to kill them, otherwise they will eat the New People. When you do this, the New People will honor you . . . They will honor you for killing the People-devouring monsters and for teaching . . . all the ways of living."

—Okanagan creation story

"You know, most Egyptians are terrified of cobras, but certain Egyptian women can deal with them. When I was once working at Tell El Fara'in [the ancient city of Buto, home of the cobra goddess Wadjet], I came across women who had names like Miriam the Egyptian or Fatima the Egyptian. If you had a cobra in your house you'd send for one of these women, called *rifaiea*, who would catch snakes by making them bite on milk-soaked cloths; then they'd pick them up and wrap them around their necks. To do this, these women would have to practice sexual abstinence and undergo purification rites for a month—and would repeat them every year—during which time they drank a thimbleful of snake venom every morning and were rubbed all over with the venom as well."

—from *The Search for Omm Sety*

"Now I can't tell the day from night,
I'm crazy as a loon.
You've got me chasin' rabbits, pullin' out my hair,
And howlin' at the moon."

—Hank Williams, "Howlin' at the Moon"

CONTENTS

ACKNOWLEDGMENTS

With gratitude to Anselm Berrigan, Ed Bowes, Michelle Ellsworth, Fast Speaking Music, Roger Green, Erika Hodges, Pat Steir, Edwin Torres, and the extremely helpful Lannan Foundation. And to Alicia Ostriker, who turned me toward Biblical Miriam. Applause to my excellent editor Paul Slovak.

And appreciation to *The Brooklyn Rail*, *Conjunctions*, *Denver Quarterly*, *Poetry*, *The Progressive*, and *Siècle 21*, in which some versions of this writing was published.

And to MaelstrÖm/ City Lights/ Mondo Di Luce for *Crépusculaire*, Bookleg #132.

"Melpomene" and "Trickster Feminism" are considered part of the ongoing Iovis Project, Book IV.

TRICKSTER FEMINISM

trick o' death

when you are sitting
with the corpse of your friend
this is what to do
when what do you do

if you are strong
make a binding of your mind
surface the body
breathe in quick breaths

huff! huff!
this is what to do
libation in small drops
on heart center
coins of ancient India on eyes
feathers and serpentine
remembrance
and open words like talismans
that shake the cosmos
as in opening a crypt
asleep too long
for death is awakening
and the alive, like you, ahunted
like "art" like "phantasm"
they will guide you
around the heart
circle around heart's cold
with drops of amrita

leave them there
of candle, frugal
or flame
can she see?
she can still hear they

say hearing is last to go
more of this is what to do
images of all you loved
to go and lastly
enterprise to repeat
acts of love, and in going
pound heart once more
dear suffragette
summon here
to outlast the misogynist
other curative wisdom
what is our speed
to know from branches of laurel
trick o' death a strategy
this is what to do

be tactful
the dead are shy
go inside them
visit their nooks & crannies
visualize their ash & impermanence

then how to start a spirit fire
play some music with your hands
sing masculine song of the mourning dove
you are alive in cosmetic time

her death chamber cooler now
stretched on the plinth
her cheek fading
you can whisper: see the syrinx,
laurel, a tuft of reeds offered
reeds like to hold you close
one hundred eyes see from inside you
no false twitch

could be nothing
going on
but seeing like this
a cut, a scar the beautiful slit
of feminine aperture

and can laugh at trick o' death
that's what you say to
a fabulous corpse
ungendered now
trick o' death
growing younger by
stuttered moment:
have no fear

she's getting out of this
into another maelstrom
or just nothing, no breathing
streets are quieter
world violence
feels less structural
lies as secrets seem truer now
you nab them
the interlocutors
blue calcite
most prominent heirloom
in color, texture
imagination of mercurial
twilight words to utter
in the doorway
the bottom of the mind
paved
smart luck
with crossroads
encryption, generation

to know you, spider
of crypt

what does the trickster say
kinetic or
clown
or
hiding so as in retreat
how many come-ons in one lifetime
you will stand in for her beauty
fend off patriarchal poetry
and your own struggle
in cultural anachronism
bombing unilaterally
nothing about
socially constituted
witch trials
women restrain or manipulate desire
face understood it must vocalize
a kiss
working a voice
(dead lady of the lake)
opposed to state apparatus
my sword! my sword!
my mirror! my mirror!
come, sirrah, come
help your mistress sleep

behind the dull glass
what face
pleasure gleam
herself
in status quo
mottled
ragged coyote

of display
acculturation text
rite's viability
bleeds
naked return?
code this
anatomical
"mothers"
dressing up like
a prince to love you
form is arbitrary
ruins hard
to
imagine
what the country wants
needles
appropriate to
need
"the people
want it"
look of the west
mysterious logos
rock on the road
the Ghent Altarpiece
and its tribulation
exemplified in the material
worship they nibbled
monsters under cartel
broken-down colonial
power
it issues forth
her disordered mouth
erotic wish
or queer?

I believe in crucible logic
harassment & insubordination
breaking through
no regulation
but performance
what is the grammar drag,
how exquisite demon feminine
not be victim
a vow, a queen
will not be plaything
you, sister, reckoning
a large-scale genome algorithm

taking you down
maelstrom
of own mind
it pulls it spins you, gender
into fragmented realities
of future past & present
a span is epic is how
every life-form is turbulent
where you are seen in
a series of guises
and some go exhaust
the void, a full place
and a sensory gate still opens
what wanted to believe
went there in a dream
of sleight of hand
shark of all cards
giving out
the tactile organs
kinesthesia like handshake
eidetic tesserae
bargained my kidney,

my spleen, my
temporal lobe
eyes in all heads
too many impostors
hacker in a past life?
how's the glitzy facade?

saying, your woman's hand has
a detour
if you just open this door
ghost was saying
your woman's bed has a detour

is true? I wonder
in red
she wears the same scarf I do
her hair is shorn,
tonsured

this is and
this is and this is
the way it looks
and this is the way it is
and this is the way she looks and
this is the way she is
this is the nimbus she is
and this is her rebus
this is the category and
this is a song of her restitution
this is the calyx and this is the individual
this is the etiquette and this is the lung
this is the shadow & abacus of hovering
a trace to count on
who will bear the weight of this tissue
this issue, hair & nails of the yogini

this is the clinical this is the invasion
this is the odds and these are the statistics
whatever you meet unexpectedly on the path
embrace,
cross purposes whenever you can
expand the road

longer limb that long extends
and this is the longer lung that extends
longer speech, she was always vocally
the longest of all
concatenation
mouthing off the longest syllable
ask and whatever you meet
and your own death, asking
this is and this is a longing
this is Ceres summoning Dame Hunger
this is Ethiopian Andromeda
or Lady Midnight's *Songs of the Four Seasons*
this is tranced attention
this is Hermaphroditus
this is a shouter, an Engine-Woman
become a midnight star, Callisto

when you are in your trouble
and turn from death
this is what to do
find the meeting place:
intersectionality
under stars
way to gnosis
saying this is the place
this is indeed the place
with many layers
lie down here

where one thrives in parity
with thieves and lovers
where one can fuck without retribution
(meet me at the edge of town)
a road out there
answer to curiosity
don't you get it?
derivative mimicry
isn't going to reflect world's
madness like she can
out of doors mimicking love or death
junction where you can go either way
and feminism is old mistress to strange
tiers of it to make you think
on death
how cold it is out on the road
making love like this
with the stars conspiratorial, hey!
they are your neighbors
slivers of twinkling form
in and out of many universes
existing in "probability space"
ice rustles, shimmers above
clouds and you are probable too
what shape, body?
with what do you inspire devotion?
how do you construct existence?
your pioneer apparatuses
your added-on
identity, a voice hits all the
registers
your conglomerations
with your timidity
with your power
your willingness to die

and cairns where we'll leave
markers for you
find the way
to love that drives you?
loosened aside a bower
down the road

little tones piling up to make a melody of
a way your various parts organize to
be here in fiction
stones can be struck
will one still sit astride
his thigh
or it hasn't started having onto you yet
heaving, hanging
bright girl
don't you get it
how they fuss you over
with love of all things mental
meant to be in your care
innermost being
insides of things, as poet feels
inner bark from a ghost tree
aspiration, and go down
and some still resting on laurels of survived
dominance look again
a factotum
a dead book perhaps
drive my sex into its covers
driven by lust outside
fear that money drives
the world down under
to shut all feeling of existence out
great mind
will I be bought by

last-ditch patriarchy
how weakens

maybe passed by here
and bowed and made offering
to corpse of rascals

stones speak of hardship
where you boil them for food
for their mineral ink magic
scribe is the biologist
new phase coming
of tones made visible
odd patches of kin
scribe is tentacular
memes of evolving feminism
and the means of it
speak your heroes, mash them
mixed with fervor of protists
how assiduously seeking truth
this is what to do
as in ways or means
and a committee meets to
make sure
a con won't push over you
force goods that enhance
misty feminine way of life
how to sell it? undiluted
disempower the girl

get down, morphing sister
get down
what are your ploys
stacking up
capitalist wiles

may they be dashed
lauded over aroma
scents of perfumed doom

avaunt idiots of compassion
and the titular rape mode of quest & scheme

what do we see? a weeping
Capitalocene
a weeping many centuries wide
vaster submersible system
it weeps
and weeps crocodile tears
a stall of state
the Mao of
hurt
the *heil* for hell
the muss of the hurt
churl
a Franco murders
a pol a pot a Papa Doc
somo, pero pino Assad
of the hurt
capital hurts

despots go down
on bite of diction
& silence of sycophants
complicit in their slimy way
attend
won't bend hearts

to abused
moans of extinction

trauma, trauma
to this poetry now

get over right now
paradox of fear
ineptitude
muscle up
find yourself in boundary
a name which means
"I have tricked you"
woman up
your paradox of betrayal

false?

didn't steal the poems,
am I not their keeper?

want to crash gates of
city, life gives
ambiguity & deceit to
old fem con to make you pay
all this curvaceous beauty
and tough sisterhood
take heart my lovely
meet me on the other edge of town
(one for lovers
this one for assassins)
dagger glints in moonlight

how many femmes can you hold
in dusk time
when it's too late
the friend the enemy
hag in retribution

how many years, an icy lore
remote that they do this to any bodies
you know they do this to women
on their rounds
and to bodies sensitive as women's
the strange, displaced the transposed the
fully realized however declaring self

expression to move,
chiasmatic,
heaven & earth
resumes holy measures
and it is a *spiritus praxis* I sing
O lordy lordy
to open your own tomb
then you're fearless
when you are both tomb
and prescient womb

go down, matrix
down, sepulcher of women
stealing your secrets
and these are the secrets I steal
innermost beings
a mesh of silicon & copper
all the pulchritude in the world

they'll beat it, meme of us: metataxis
the oligarch is in charge
is at it metabolically and has to go
we make him go

grasses will hide and rejoice
we make him go
please learn this before you leave the earth
rout plights to bury the wild girl

women in abstraction thinning
facedown ones
they do rise
in disguise of agenda
what is the ploy?
a strange miasma. . . .
catch him
make him go
from our body of light
though we be trickster shadow
a scented elixir
drank the
what is it?
wordless amrita?
without word
crossroads will make you stand tall
in your architecture of chance
"down the rabbit hole"
you rise out the other side
you survive

feminism is your ploy,
ofttimes retired
come out now
not disenfranchised
nor abandoned
nay obsolete
how many you go con
bruited lab death of feminism?

when you sit with
the corpse of your world
let it shut its corpse

rabbit is in the moon
illusion's illusions strumming on

being around voice
jumping thrice over coyote
trick o' death

take down the big horrible men
destroy them in their icy sleeves
cuff them
not you brethren but impostors
and their minions
who cater and mew and shuffle

just so you know what stage femme
is on evolving
its fluid body
its principle
the crossroads can't nail you down
to ignorance
but it's a promise
meets you there
speculating
with choice & impetus
which way the wind blows
avenge all deaths of hers
poet-thief
drive the stake in

denouement

Patriarchal Poetry might be withstood.
Patriarchal Poetry at peace.
Patriarchal Poetry a piece.
Patriarchal Poetry in peace.
Patriarchal Poetry in pieces.

—*Gertrude Stein*

And the day would be proud of itself going on as if it hadn't already collapsed, had not been destroyed, riven, all the people mad and metabolically downcast. It's around the eyes. It's around the hearts. The city was reeling. People were coming out to the street. In the way they wanted to see where the big guy lived and boasted so as to mock the event. It wasn't over. It wasn't going to rest. The guy was not real as the day as the year the century the epoch shared, was not real the tribulation he ensued, was not real but it was that affect that mattered: *what would suffer.* It was the warmest year on record as if that wasn't enough to make some citizens pause and pausing resist and if resisting insist on being heard and calibrated so that measures were taken round the clock, ice caps photographed melting and all the rest, a pole away from accountability. How ugly would it go?

Resistance. Had to resist. Ward off. Deflect. Exorcise. Defy. Apotropaic experiments to shift tone & danger. *Apo*, away, *trepein*, to turn. Make the day an amulet. And there were women everywhere across the land, children women, and girl women and they women and fluid women and men who were women and boy women and women from the past on the tongues of mind & ear and images of women everywhere: ancestor women. Out on the streets. And everyone woman that day. I am woman they said. And it had already happened if you stopped to think. Winning in maenad heaven, but could earthly heart hold? The day said I am woman. The day got up and walked this far then paused to take stock. It was the last chance to be observant and cry and stomp and take stock. What worth if not be accountable. It would be theater, a spectacle, come pay, or come lie down in fluid bosom of woe mankind.

Remember the Kabuki you saw imitating resolution between a sword and a fox, a country and its honor? How things & animals become agents of plot & resolve. Last straws of honor. Sword resists, now broken on its back. Wild animal comes in peace. New maps, treaties, synapse. And blue of sky—midnight blue—was invoked in the shroud that draped the mobster's chair where he sat timeless waiting for the play to begin. He was temporarily on pause, a mechanism that played to its own tune of false entitlement. Fake rhythm not in tune with the spheres. But kicks in. We were it. Played upon. Blink of demon eye oscillating over doomed electorate. And we were becoming shroud of gray, rough warp & woof. Signals collapse of silken worlds, now static, unravel. We'll reboot *Silky damp dark of the labyrinth.* Going down. Maybe one could still supplicate. Take back founding myth of Americas: evil of the Feminine.

Centuries might wake up spin out stories of what this got built on or if what wasn't liable was what unleashed in damage and you have to say it is severe this time. Male body how it dominates since 3000 BC in Sumer Tiamat's monsters. Blowback, perturbation this time. Traps of appetite. Weather & addiction. Rogue nukes. Say it to remind how the time might go on as theater of dreams. Of signs of this time. The signals go weirder and you are on assignment every angle of the street. Every minute every day: avert, deflect. Every pilgrim theory is false and unsustainable in inclement weather. In the dream you stand in front of an ornate gate but only by dancing does it open. Glamorous women had been fasting with games of break & entry, disguised as beggars to confuse the upper echelons. But they continue to move phenomenologically, no longer objects/subjects of phallic desire. This time, this time. Apocalypse, this time, this time.

She had been up on Fifth Avenue mumbling mantras of pacifying enriching magnetizing and destroying as she circles the tower, giving wide berth. *Om Man Be Gone Om Man Be Gone Om Con Con Be Gone.* She gathers wealth of mind and she invokes black Maria & No Land & Alystyre & Mineb & Eline. And Natalia & Eva & queer Serene. Selah & Tonya & mysterious HR. And witness material richness as she gazes with woman's gaze into the holiday windows. It isn't holiday gaze anymore. It is incinerator, dungeon, risk, a bludgeon. It is tribulation, it is prelude to tract of pleas to the Gorgon and her two lionesses mounted on Aegis & shield of Athena, to Saint Brigid, to exorcism and all heresies of women. To Wenet, Lady of the Hour, with raised scepter to grate souls. It is the antinomian gaze of the gulag. Prelude into twilight an irreparability for shimmering crystals, the glimmer-edge of baubles & adornment. To Wadjet, her cobra trance.

Earlier the carillon rang clear from a sanctuary on Fifty-Third Street. And people cheered and felt tones ringing inside their selves and sleeves of themselves which gave further power to rebuke a normalization habit wanted to demand of them, people, sentient-abiding people. Go hide? We were in modest rain gear & coats of wool made for long treks across mountains. Nights in front of a fire, watching patterns in flames play out a sciamachy, and she renewed her practice of circling, of surrounding, of chanting. She remembered the flood she was inside of might return. The closeness of fire & water & ice & breaks in the ground of Earth waiting until we be gone. What other Earth have you ever known? Elements dance in collusion. What sophisticated algorithms could hold in a tempest. Earth trying to tell us something. And maybe we could rouse the rabble. And maybe we could have a parable about craving soil under avenues, hope & fear. Times of the chthonic.

How to think. Wisps on screens of earth-mind as out of battle. Imprinted there for future entanglement. Memory returns. And when one dies or drowns the image bobs up to light, a hologram, one who traveled to the bottom of the pond to meet a friend. Or one who would rise from the center of the meadow, a warrior holds mewling baby, semblance of babes everywhere under siege. Clang out the words: reeks of genocide. How FEMA came to inspect the damage, polite and politic. How con inside wants more than they give because they take so much of us. Our fear which is ground up and reconstituted with malice including a speeding on of raids, of unconstitutional praxis. Break down the door. Give me a better word for ~~torture~~ for ~~genocide~~ for ~~minimalism~~ for exhaustion in a lack of power to move ethical clocks forward. Over soon in catastrophe of ~~craving~~. I will write that myself: reminder to realign the world.

Who goes down to write? Where to run to write? What is a "safety net" tonight? Watch Nasdaq soar. Listening to pundits saying what you know better than they do. How many cots available in the basement of the reformed church in Queens. Where harbor of our energy, hard-earned money, treasure & blood. How to exact spiritual synapse of dailiness and the accretion of years of psyops. On borrowed time? Innocent in our refrains, repetitions of received knowledge. Who would be suffragette and thinking about modes of survival more and more and not be wiser. What we inhabited now, shadow war. From a height a great widening from a height a slow widening, who might be watching inside thinking, a self-presumed one in a place of widening polemic. "I used to compare becoming a feminist to jumping off a building and deciding halfway down it wasn't such a good idea," said Lucy Lippard in a great widening.

Musing on the tracks where trains deliver plutonium for nuclear warheads that infect our world. Seepage in the water that will go on long after species morphs to another stardust in the lungs of the wind of the windblown world of the establishing toxins invisible particles in the interstices every fissure breathes where does one not breathe although it will be unnecessary to breathe what one imagines when that will not be the mechanism shopping around for the right fixing new technologies to give over breathing with acculturated lungs and perhaps as women take their lungs into a hiding place and move deeper underground you will wonder is breathing like a corner of a book when your breath stops the lines are so beautiful? Obsolete words like "hiddenness." You stalk the air its hiddenness. You choke in Delhi, you choke in Kolkata, take a hit in Kathmandu.

No fixed transhistorical, no fixed feminine, no fixed constituents cut through this body of difference. Meant saying collectively it's normal survival to decipher a pedestal binding you to come down from o willingly no fixed irreducible ground. Class, ethnicity, nationality, no fixed ground. Body is inadequate concept although I love you body whatever you are whoever you are whatever you are I love you body. I love you body I love you suffering body living in an animation of Eros whatever you are everything is art everything is erotics of engagement everything is war everything is reason or dressing it up and coming back from reading you who does this to me a plot in a book tucked in my brain a boundary to cross keep reading inside shape of a crenellated world you still can't rule. But trying. Drink antidote—thimbleful of plutonium—each mutating morn.

Threat growing taller because it was moving up from water, safe from water as it widens, water widens. Then water surrounds. The floods were living water, surrounds. Sounding and far from desert. Or asked to be. Then presumed. Then in genome laboratory. Surrounding and gathered everywhere. Her fierce nakedness, her stare. Her animal head. Because she would have better instinct in simplicity of a paranoid animal or happy harmony. Deflect all toxins now. Bunnies in the yard, jay in the locust tree, fox down the road, bear spotted out by the chickens. Antidote for a hunter-gatherer world. A trapdoor designed for you alone could anyone else enter here, cross a walk, step for the size of walking would it be useful in crossing to think about? About anyone else? And all your robotic things. Simple things to own to get by. Your wounds, your hurricanes, your artifacts. Identities to get by. Genders try you on.

The biggest failure was the predator big guy who abuses women. The phony puritan was at it again, brandishing trash from the rooftop. The city was falling. I kept circling like an assassin, weaving in resistance with all the mammals with mind-protecting mantras. A temple of last reckoning. Easy to forget who you are long days under siege. History will decide moments, but you live them. Crossroads beyond identity you have to go to stake for your fractured land. Place where forces gather. They could put you away, rights stripped down, murder you. Shadowy nimble trickster comes mysteriously out of twilight, walking backward, walking sideways and flying in air too. Scrying the tracks & flight patterns you will come to when we've forgotten how to read: *Rescue*.

crepuscular

où l'artiste crie de frayeur avant d'être vaincu.

—*Baudelaire*

Code your language and escape.

They won't find you.

I made them up.

I made the words and then could hide them.

They won't find you who are words.

Hiding in twilight.

Stay hidden.

A sensual twilight.

Cartouche & star pattern in a long format.

In any language.

Conceal your heresy.

Bright colors, repeating motifs.

Practice your *pradakshina*, holy circumambulation.

Around the corner from the cops, the guards, the hounds.

I made them up, my images seeking defiance.

Future suffragette
move closer,
her trial a trail of
ratification
and progress.
Never halt,
more words.

Hidden in glazed ceramics.

Hidden in the thirteenth century.

A tympanic membrane.

I made them a code with elaborate plumage.

Where the letters & digits sprout wings.

Grow feathers, making them sleek and haughty.

Help, avian, off the page.

We are all our sisters, an entangled codex.

Help us, Furdausi of Tus.

A dark pride.

The wives are trembling.

Justice, expediency.
Suffragette argues,
a speech of any
one woman's life.
Would a ballot
protect you?

Iran is my poem today.

Hide in the calligraphy of desire & devotion.

Rise and fly in the signatures of space / time.

The sigil of adoration.

Wisdom of Lemurian Angels.

Vox of code sings to you in deregulated time.

Be ready though you languish in new temper's fluency.

Be ready although you fight for exuberance.

You card arises, be ready, this rebellious season.

Ancient with text, no muzzle on purpose.

Would be unconditional in Edenic time.

The tarot culls then falls.

A seal across your lips

Ancient with text that has no design but desire.

It puzzles its male adversaries.

Get ready, you are the force majeure.

You better reawaken.

The solstice strengthens you.

Equinox will lift your cloak at dawn.

The skirts of all tribes will find alignment.

Line up in an astral dance.

The notion is to secede from vocabulary they give you.

Force Arcane: linguistic hand guides you.

Through birth and its constraints.

Words like "location," "stucco," "private," "coming to get you."

Resounding.
　And family.
I cannot eat or
　wear the money
he brings home
　each payday.

That will pick up pieces for all women.

New Shechinahs, the glass shatters.

Words like "futurity," like "pagan," like "heresy" resound.

The shell game continues finding its small proof.

Excavators of Afrasiyab suggest many walls.

Crepuscular in a season as escape from hell.

You are being tested, all your orality your mockery.

Memorize sighs & plans for survival.

You are being tested in a lioness-mouth.

With your eyes on "negentropy," on "survival."

All your utopias of stasis afire.

You are being tested.

Gather ashes for the twilight of protest.

From the fire, force majeure.

Train the acolytes.

They lean into the blessings of the full moon.

Poetry is finally visible in civil defense.

Practice disobedience as a coven might.

Give me political
    status.
I do not eat the home.
I cannot eat
    the house.

I will lie down and
    read my books.
I will write
    another tractus.
A long upswing
    panting for freedom.

Your tears are the dialectic of all truth now.

Force majeure bubbling up from the cauldron.

Can you read poetry in water?

In fire?

Mysterious presence in the urban twilight.

Will poetry quench thirst in revolutionary night?

Find text or purpose here?

Inscribed on Emma Goldman's activist bones.

Welcome to a gilded age coming down.

There was history of thirst.

Water wars in the hinterlands.

All the soldiers in moist womanhood.

Milk-soaked clothes catching cobras.

Come to us now, love of the serpent.

The honcho is writing it down.

With his honcho women.

If he differ how they
differ from
each other.
From men.
The great sanctuary
is the gate
of women.

Watch out!

You will be singled out, Saisara the Grinning One.

Eleusinian underworld goddess.

Needing auscultation.

What is my musical disorder?

How may I sound my feet & hands?

How may I clasp the code and sing?

It was the last white stand to hold women down.

A repertoire of new decrees.

Saudi sisters behind the wheel.

The allegory always waiting is for those coming after.

The algorithms are secret and not understood by all.

Telos! Telos!

Those who study
  the sturdy oak
about which
  the ivy clings
find it dead at the top.

Or could be used against you.

Invoke epopteia, "the having been seen."

You were known for your advocacy, your rasp.

To stabilize the state.

For the people who gathered to be poets again.

Whirred, conjured. Drank elixir.

Did the evening ceremony before light faded.

Made the ritual up: in eight dimensions.

Light coming through the lattice.

Face of filigree, and her hennaed hand.

I made them up: queen-size dimensions.

One: was where things ended.

They had been in the world thousands of years.

Two: was that they buffeted against where the scholars leaned.

Three: they were the new translators, gaining ground.

As they waited for the final mysteries.

Four: tumult in the street. Kompromat!

Auspicious alignment of stars.

Five: Not ours! Not ours!

Not our phoenix.

Not our dragon.

And people were alive but bent.

Stunned in the face of "it," monstrous memory.

Women hugged their astrolabes all over the world.

And their cunning faces genuflected over their hearts.

Suffragette minimus
walks,
Suffragette minimus
shows up,
Suffragette minimus
attempts
to convince the
fence-sitter.

As if strumming lyres.

Six: some held cloth with texts sewn of red thread.

Red of desire, red of blood. Fooling you about blood.

Seven: a possible intervention, and could you invoke law.

You would write a book of law.

Silence, when no one heeded words.

Eight: a ceremonial journey by condemned sovereign and her minions.

What realm of hell?

Even the olive trees had not heard lamentation.

And the transgendered one invented a new language.

It was mystic it was "fluid" it was "ziggurat."

Suffragette notes
the new
immigrants
use Sunday
for recreation.
They drink?
Make merry?

"Telesterion."

It was *visio beatifica*.

You would know in time as you turned facing the new world.

Assassins in the wings, wait for instructions.

They were neutral or so they said.

This was a code where women meant infinity.

Where you have nothing to lose.

We were on Tibetan translucent time.

And in Demeter's dawn time.

By the virgin wall.

The wall of flowers.

A kind of muscle at your back.

Made the polemic day into night.

Made it: night into day.

A membrane trembles.

Lycosura in cosmic mantle with her closed basket.

Within, instruments of poetry.

A sweet time for lovers in song.

Language softens in the instruction manual.

In the *cista mystica*.

Thank you poets.

You rescued our minds.

Turned grief into tenderness.

Into world of tangible things.

A membrane grows porous.

Women work
outside the home,
they rarely live
in a big house
on tree-lined streets,
but prefer the
overcrowded
tenements.

Morphs in cunning ways, sexual promise.

You better grab the time you have.

Never have this time again.

And then you may take leave, depart.

But do this nightly in riding the blast.

Ingest ergot and ride your words.

Become the gallows humor.

Of this disambiguation am a kind of hieroglyph.

Strike with words.

Strike with walkout power, a new stylus, boycott.

Pathetic fallacies not working in the towers of gold.

Thrones crippled in the psyche of oligarchs.

Turn the corner, more to do, under breath.

The code was a way to accumulate quick assets.

Used by the benevolent socialist moles underground.

Riding up the queer conversion elevator to become more queer.

The observers who track your status, who have your "number."

Prescience of animals because they could abet the holocaust.

They prefer
tenements
   in which
Mother could
rarely be Queen
of her home.
Suffragettes
note this
   and complain.

Translated by their emotions and want to help too.

But who listens?

Do not queer the deal.

Crepuscular was a lonely bell.

Crepuscular was quid pro quo.

I loved all the bodies of my loves.

Do not harm the twilight that saves you.

Crepuscular knew the language of business.

Of title & exchange.

What is this to the Sixth Extinction?

Mess in the hallways?

Corridors of more men?

"I" was code for the hacker I am.

Be true and all the colors.

Be wild and all the colors.

I would magnetize and destroy my own uniform.

I walked the pavements in a new skin.

That we walk free, chanting "Resist, resist om ah con be gone."

And help the
   poor immigrant.
      Suffragette
   will speak.
Suffragette minimus
   complains of steerage.
   Compliant,
      literacy test?
   Debates.
Taxpayers.

Quick alignment.

New people were honing their chatter.

Their cameras were on the prize, the clever abomination.

Onstage with fascist enterprise.

They were metastasizing in every corner.

Vituperative talk shows held the days.

Escape hatches on two sides of town.

Dug into the earth.

Sanctuary! Sanctuary!

Took umbrage at rudeness of patriarchs.

Dashed their brains into the night.

Not ours! Not ours!

Dash mental fixation into the night.

Circumambulated the zones at twilight, again.

Day after day, protocol demands poetry.

I come back one hundred years to do this, again.

Because we are already out of the cave.

Force Arcane: come out now.

Standing alone.
  Suffragette maximus.
Standing in unison.
  Foreign borners
joining suffrage
  organizations.
Numbers swell.

You are under all of us.

All the feminine, all the left-hand paths.

"Learn what rhythm holds us."

Shadow on the other side of heart.

And we are circling the tower.

Adjudicating the story.

This time of membrane, of beauty, of woe.

People are equal, get ready.

They were everywhere, racist impostors.

Looming in their tax-deductible paradises.

Arriving in luxury cars.

Ugly caskets of doom.

They are not kind.

They want my city.

The new brokers of desire & greed.

I made them up: wheedling brokers.

It was twilight, a new alchemy for the time.

Tower is fake gilded age.

O my workers!
How do we categorize
    the impact of
the black man?
Abolition a cause,
    and surely, abolition
the cause.

Progressive era,
    a secret like Eleusis.
Eleusis embellishing
    the ranks . . .
Eleusis coming to
suffrage.

Anything goes in the old town: Nueva York.

Diffused light.

Below horizon.

Dim illumination.

State of obscurity.

Of mantic mind.

Of absurdity.

Resist in twilight.

Don't pour myrrh over my head.

Or batter me with fillets of wood.

Here at the day, end of this day.

My arcane, a secret evolution.

With a "hat with the shape of the infinite."

A force under the surface.

A lion that comes out of her sex, roaring.

A dialectic, a rattle, a song.

Sing to me, a purpose.

Do not forget orality of wild purpose.

Suffragette
inside
your pin.
Your palm.
You made us
a tongue,
Suffragette.

Do not forget the false memory of the world.

Twilight becomes true memory summoned by roaring.

mash de beauvoir

"Her destiny is inside her scattered in
cities already built." Supple ripples of
creed. This is about light too bright,
about architecture's brusque tension.
This is a knitting recipe. This is more
eyeglass invention than has eyes for.
Melancholy to conquer a new lover. A
woman wants to knock down fruit from
a tree. Test your own power. What is her
hand in a river. Swept by breath that
animates her. This is the fruit of
suffering, hanging bodies lest you
forget. You must never forget pleasure
in women in sex a "magic spell." You
must never forget cruelty in women,
immanence and repetition. Through
such action grasp smoke. Pride is in the
word "liberation" if blood were only
food. Struggle. Intoxication. Don't spill.
This was all deduced from the topic
"he." Deduced from monsters. This is
about interlocutors. The leaf cutters
would stay on track. Then start all over.
Harvest the growth spurt. Harbor
the mold, fight memories of wartime
girlhood. Smile in a mirror. This is
sovereign on a hillside, up-tempo.
Dipping a hand in the river.
Contumacious. To conquer, unite. Have
reciprocity, tract of caprice. The "he"
posits strands of RNA, small vehicles,
paths to them. And he is existent. But
this then the next step. Follicles of "he."
Liquidity. "Old is life's parody." Sparks.

Start all over in revolution. Between
them for a new future. She changed her
mind about breasts. Life is interested in
posterity. He changed her mind about
pleasure. Unlimited. Shining shoes.
Does blur. Somewhere between others.
Virile steadfastness in French harmony.
Her. Others. At least touched a trace of.
This is smell of the lover. The subject
was to be "those who coddle themselves
make hay." Species available. Days and
nights, side by side would be the
outcome. Not the body she's born to.
Quite opposite. This is about light too
dark. Crawls like a baby. This was in
access of. Hoist the tracing mirage.
Don't make an object yet. When absent
radical transformation of the cortex, the
witness reports: "Went to the people."
So the topic gets resolved if we read
further in *aporia*. Kiss behind a door.
Celibate solitude. Mores of immutable
species. Carnal singularity. Adviser to
an older woman: If they rest, do not
discuss false unions. We want
conclusion, mixing a remedy to wake up
by. Aim for sky. Are dice loaded?
Sometimes. Hegel please agree. Let's
refute. Always. Doll as double. Fault
amplified. Pleasure softens the better
angel. Myriad effusion. Preserve the
parallel. The woman wants to sign off
sky. And be done. Profusion. This above
was an example of imaginary. A woman
was evaluated. "Made for another
planet." "On the other hand, she kept

writing." Below: subjectivity means competition. "Sex is autonomy. Comes with access." Argue: Alchemy made totality. The notion of . . . insufficient. The apparatus says sheer repetition. Use. Emanates. Quest for being hormone. You can get shots you know. Her dark hair rolled. Her body is a kind of salt on the silk road. To the side: ritual after mating. There is a drugstore. Paved with gold. Play a role here. On average, smaller difference in larynx brings less voice. Less calcium salt. Her skeleton is thinner. Her forms are rounder. Things change: less hemoglobin. Neptune laughter in ear, votive shell. Peripherally nervous. Excitation. If a ground, then value. Is it the Bolsheviks' fault? Reach for the vitamin. Inject. "Whatever happens, don't cry. If you give way to tears, sad rebuttal." Example: so violence holds and grants more food. Statistics how many. Story of hiding glyphs in philosophy. (This is the point I'm making!) Needing the sorcerer to read them. The existent is a sexed body. Lines and dots. Series is warning. Code for book. Not a color line. Mosaic, take as given. If a male were to be proud. A sorcerer is a kind being, just transfer, then transformer. The sorcerer wears shoes in the city. Once a sorcerer tread on hot coals. She sucks out toxins. Caution. Herein lie weakness. "Don't forbid." "Know difference." "Density, this is endangerment." "I would dress in Mummy's lace." Prepare a ruse. These were examples of logic and inference. Sentence: "His waking had improved if I would wait." Sentence: "Poor cloistered being who makes holes of sadness." Sentence: "Empty dress thrown down on a floor for the man to seize and wear." Need more examples. Make the point. This was an example for elder restless ♀. Conclusion in taste or habit of solitude. Frenzy of tears and attitude. Conclusion in the new rebuttal: Everything goes wrong when you don't want to come in second. In March of this common era Nimrud was destroyed. The fourth capital of the Assyrians went down four days later. Year of our lord's sentence: "Parasite of the rich bourgeoisie, feelings of brotherhood?" Public confession. Sisters charge. Change into elementary social call. Or "don't weep." Become our own volcano. "The desire to protect and rock in her arms a soft object made of flesh is shared with the lesbian."

clytemnestra's body polis ticks

Sensemayá, the snake
sensemayá
Sensemayá, with its eyes,
sensemayá . . .
            —*Nicolás Guillén*

I'd rather be a Cyborg than a
Goddess.
            —*Donna Haraway*

Be such a strong fact
        You would sleep
            of those I kill

Milk running over

Name a variant of "scheme"

To act not hurt? A body

Render it barren, body's politic

Nor spill dripping rain
        Athene demands *Turn it up*

The hungry Syrians

and who is up for rule?
A *labrys*, the double-headed
ax for thought

Carnage for thought

Suffer eclipse
        can't see can't see the syndicates
        but see their murder spill forth

For want of a brain
        yet I have without wine
succumbed this crazy politic

Unhooked the little-box-world

Men are stumping their speeches

White bodies in the horror-void
        whose desiccated lips spew oil

I can't be media for want of a brain

Stains set you free after vetting
        secret pacts & deals
go crazy with conspiracy

I always vote beside the hearth
        keep my house alive
be not a murderer of sleep

Bloc at the feet, heart, eyes

For want of a brain stem
    the nukes go free

All my arrows were the candidates

Ur-this, the ur-that, ur-person

Aggrandizement

The self goes down. . . .
In augury with a nuked family body

For want of a society the bees run free
For want of a fibula the world strums

Sisters elect of our wonder; a barker:
    pearls and blue beads
cobalt stuff, a prison outfit

For want of obstruction
    run free, O body in chains
and the other one had a cuff link perhaps

Will others don?
Will swear?

Keep an upright way, Amerika

Pancake makeup & pundits
And sway to a better idea?

Make no mistake
  when greater disaster comes
    robber baron is all you are

Helm of my psychic state will not go gentle

Out of the riches, yet
    mid-grips for the temps on strike in Michigan

This is not a red state
This is the seat of Pallas

Alive in the estates of the father

Enough, cry hold, poison darts

and they come from a mocking tree
in ritual misadventure
        upon all who stroll across oaths

Hunted beast slips from our nets

Gone to *sambhogakaya*,
        timeless body of light

Won't sleep with me no more no more no more
    for want of a bed

Charioteers go on strike
    for want of a whip

Mount the statue of Athene
        and her plebes, suckle at bitter breast

Eyes with blood
who cannot see it's plain to see

Stain & power, the activist streets
Receive your call

In secrecy of night
    spring clear for want of an ear

Hear what it calls to all minions
    resist retort reclaim

For want of a tongue
        the world crumbles

You cannot get my dream,
    Furies
            for want of imagination

Whimper you must

For want of an ark
  you cannot get me an ark

For want of the sea
For want of my solace
a kind of dramaturgy

Go Hermes
    help me pour these lustral
    waters

Or get up, feet
    for want of a mother-snake
Or hound whose thought of hunting has no shape

Sic 'em
Let go, bloodshot breath
Vital's heat

The dumb TV waken, speak severally
  no more promises

In the town hall
you want plurality

Try a whole matricidal chorus
      pumped up for this

For want of a forum
let stabbing voice of the Etruscan speak

Let her breathe
A single ballot can restore a tree house

O god of the younger generation
under pods a future cruelty

Serpent power of sinewy cruelty
or staggering beast wore out its time . . .

"Fuck land and bring your ton of hatred upon it!"

Tyranny not bring your bulk of
        hatred on anything

Really, but
civility? I promise you a void

I promise you a place
in the sacrosanct booth

Jagged loners eat the seeds

Or I'll accept all devotions by you, citizens

(Медведь не тро́нет мёртвое те́ло.)
A bear will not touch a dead body.

melpomene

steatite limestone calcite . . .
       when the mountains pry us apart

*There had been catastrophe. There would be catastrophe. The time in
which a man lived was a whirl or drift in a great sea that might rise out of
itself into a roaring end of things.*

*What returned to my thought as I began work this morning was the reve-
lation of the stars. For the dream Muriel Rukeyser, the Poetess of the
major arcana of my own dream-tarot, took us out to see the night sky. All
the stars of the cosmos had come forth from the remotest regions into the
visible. At first I was struck by the brilliance of Orion, but as I looked the
field was crowded with stars, dense cells of images and then almost ani-
mal constellations of the night sky. It was as if we saw the whole over-
populated species of Man, and in that congregation of the living and
dead, the visible and the invisible members of the whole, we began to
make out patterns of men, animal entities whose cells were living souls.*

*"We see these skies here," the Poetess said, "because we are very close to
the destruction of the world."*

                                   —*Robert Duncan,* The H.D. Book

against catastrophe. In front of it

to placate
to scorn
small creature breathes life or
a sea urchin told me this from the vine
our symbiogenesis speaks

small and slithery
how they stink! the child said

poked, will it laugh

give out
various Venuses, Penates
household gods inside
place of refuge, protection

not a bridge for a tomb
end that is imploded event
fable to diminish all fables

serpentine roads to Damascus

odd how holiest of places
turned hells

a tragic muse warns you away

mammoth ivory, entwined antlers
blue moons, slant of time, of change

wandering once—those hipster planets
seem cooler—in scorn, to road our way

awaiting their own crimped extinction

did we he they thy you who what
did I me them she it
ever say it would be easy?
expedient, no fixed determinator
in metaphysic?
work by the sweat of brow moment, dormant
replicant at ready, this is the antithesis reality

mist in the cosmos ventilator at ready
stones fall on the earth
was the Word *before* this
or all aural a ready?

a fascist salute
loud *at ready*?

sound turned up
as science turns down a notch
to match warming rejection

no verification without apparatus
extend tears
art over art over an overt art
acoustic yet her silence shivers

at the ready?

wasn't it a sly detriment
constellations & tears?
she had a steel bracelet (read *torture*)
round her waist,
hot metal scale positioned above the head
horns butted forth, Ram forcing a
mechanism of the Sagittarian turned monster
all fortunes fell down
of speed of movement, of
whirling system made
tender when we held stem of scope
as tender might thrive outside the planet terrarium
and point made about wealth of nations
look there, weapons of doom
deflagrations, points—looking there
weirder graces, vexed Melpomene

under sites of AI recognition construction
conflagrations that posit mind
back to scope & privilege
that there should be a consciousness in the first place
skandha or heaps of *abhidharma* to reckon
as ego builds her palace on shaky ground
metabolically, needing tenderer bird wing shelter
else predator eagle hawk crow devours
in her depiction of self, of agency

tracked three long days when you were epic
when you were divination
when you read runes
dialectics & tragedy
gamboled with pronged antelope
on way to Yellow Mountain
see yourself prolonged in language .

Kurdish, riot grrrl
hijab as act of resistance
ruse to subvert burlesque clothing
or war, death, & burial, are you ready?

saboteur on the wild side
before the technology told you where you are
where you stop to protest under surveillance: Tibet
or mourn stateless Rohinga
and I was in the condition of *tummo*, warmed in sub-zero life
which means literally "fierce woman"
and inner fire:
candali

to cozy up a mountain
walk backward into the gyre

pulverized by refrain. I . . . . . .
by frustration, I . . . . . .
women marching, women study marching
in eruption & pulse of despairing peoples
one stops for
in metro
reconstruction of a good idea, exponentially
that we are impermanent that we suffer, that
our thoughts don't own us
thoughts to touch what? insight?
undocumented workers' rights?
or of more sinewy hybrid color made
the beings within holding their *terma*-treasure close:
little Rinpoches dancing within a bubble holding other
dancing Rinpoches in a bubble holding others
their red hats aflame
small diagrams of subatomic pathways
stretch for miles, chains of bubbles
luminous green juice pulsing through veins
metabolically welcomed into
connective tissue
to rest like monkeys off the back
another three days in cave
pallet on the ground
jackals sounding
waxen wick of the yak candle
tapering down
character in your own detoxification myth
and survival perhaps around the margins
ornate spectacle of sacred text
codex of peaceable kingdoms
leaping hares flowering vines
how many knots in your magic carpet?

fiftieth anniversary of Six-Day War
never too late
with darts with hearts
combing desert for relief
collapsed moment

birds travel in intricate weave through seven valleys
the quest—*talab*—leads to annihilation—*fana*—
rings of dervishes perform the celestial dance
as an artist considers the fabricated stars as points on a compass

nuclear sleeves are my emotions
reverence, trepidation, intoxication
impasse
live inside their form

the calligrapher signed his name here
"Sultan Mohammed"
and the work was a *safina* or *bayez*
translated as "ship" or "vessel"
and by extension "ARK"
she mounts it

manuscript is carrier of assemblages of texts
vehicular vestigial markers—
tuck them in my sash or up a sleeve
spy on myself
false prophet?
what did you ever really renounce?
flying over trees
a djinni you are
before you fought hard and laid down arms for
poetry, cut teeth on
divination
its cerebral motion

eat this augury of little bones!
and the sticks scatter
and you pick them up gingerly
not to inhibit the spontaneous arrangement
unvocalized
deadly, erotic perhaps
signals with no destination
and universes on all sides pressing in
on your curiosity
is it the symmetry you embrace
chaotic multiverse?
both in the potential salute
does truth touch a Higgs boson?

conversion to a mirror of modernity
action itself we drone
points no danger into true danger
substitute a dirge for us
tragic muse

you are empty, useless in late capitalism
mimic yourself with words
inverted celebrity
fractal down at mouth
you better have fear
you are no one in this abyss
of the obvious ways you manipulate
death
for that would deprive you of
mantic power
inscribed blossom
the way you might etch on soft clay
tablets bend to meet your style
ruining the future with zenobiotic chemicals

erotic posture: polynuclear aromatic hydrocarbons
labial poem mouth: mining
hole in the universe: leaching
or as in conversation
scribed our discourse
where we were old lovers
that way in
unfolding I mean
loops on itself logics
was deep-set eye of blue
heralded you, deep-set blue
and way into you
was an epicanthic fold
suggests scripted curve
a signature could be a tent
all take shelter under, body

radical shift in the biosphere
hologram of a fourth-dimension star
on the edge of a black hole
infrastructure in mesocosmic form
make your exchanges over space

it, she said, is witch's resolve
little hut of sacred sativa
in the Terrapin store
rituals against rampant misogyny
radiant, resolute
here's a picture of a new "outing"
a person at podium not enough
to bring love back into the world
as levied off your chance
someone suffers the come-ons
a sensual surface that will be revealed
at whose expense: assault

not everyone with the same library
if you enter the password
"enchantment"
will center the outcome
and you pass iris test?

and recognized,
the mirror helps out
as you check your dream-pelt
back of the head the neck can only turn so far to
guess at identity
what could it be?
guess!
can you return my animal head
to its orient?

moments like these lead women, timbrels sounding
across the Sea of Galilee

women of sports collaborate, win a sexual strike
until husbands make peace
and end the Peloponnesian War

Tamra pretends to be a prostitute.

Researchers now working on military robots seem especially eager to
ransack the biological world for elegant solutions to the design problems
that have to be overcome. There is a snake-shaped robot that can rear itself
up in the grass when it wants to scan its surroundings. Tiny surveillance
robots scuttle up walls like bugs, and robot flyers flap their wings. The
Navy is testing submersibles that swim like fish. Researchers in the UK
have developed a robot whose sensors mimic rat whiskers—since so far no
engineer has managed to come up with a sensory system that is better at
navigating in total darkness.

feel it in the weather. not trumpet cause, which is anarcho-Buddhist-socialist-feminist-eco poethics. Call out Poetess Rukeyser. The goddess is dead. But "ess" in "stress" dead?

Inestimable
Duress
Etched in access
Adroitness
In sullenness
Etched with scars starless
Stringent
Sumptuous
Without motive
Without lust
Motionless for a moment
Progress, its essence
Its essential foil
& misnomer
The "ess" or oarlessness, or rudderlessness
Take the drift of
Capriciousness
A blameless eldress
Where I digress caress me
The "ess" of secretion
The scorpion on its rounds
You are sentiment under
keenness, kindness
ess dragging essential into existence
before annulled in eminence
before it becomes essence

existence exposed

could hold you
could wait? ess nagging essential
holds you, inestimable . . .

inspected by gremlins in white nurse dresses
who want to see if the stone could be removed

cut by a knife?
could be surgically removed from a corpse

How terrible is the advent of mutilated Aphrodite!

If we were truly cyborgian—human/animal/machine although born
from *militarism and patriarchal capital*—could we inhabit a world
without genesis perhaps, a world without end?

Dear Extremophile:
My larynx instructs me thus, proclaims a vocal imagination & trust. Was
Homo ergaster the first hominid to vocalize? And what did she say? The
larynx descended. We have an L-shaped vocal tract. And how phonemes
may also be produced on the outside of the body. Language is not a
separate adaptation but an internal aspect of some much wider symbolic
culture. Or where you find human you find poetry and capacity for song
and impulse gathered from the rambunctious animal that sways and
sings in ur-sound and body motion. Biopoetics. Oikos-Symbiosis.
Something catches on. Something is catching on. The slime molds! L is
for language, L is for love.

What myth stalks my imagination?

Dear Extremophile:
What I learned: nature was not pure unchanging, there was no "real
balance"

What I noticed: that I might "catch on" to noticing

What I learned: Pythagoras was always re: approximations

Nature was an ocean inside me. Liquidity & detail.

Knew a way: Aristarchus, Galileo, Giordano Bruno

Animal entities were pressing their bodies against me in the form of the ancient panthera

Do you need a windwoman to know which way the weather blows?

All binaries in question:

> *esprit/corps*
> *animal/humain*
> *organisme/machine*
> *la nature/culture*
> *public/privé*
> *le domicile/lieu de travail*
> *mâle/femelle*
> *artiste/carriériste*
> *la vie/économique*

All dispersed all broken down, reconfigured, interpolated upon, folded, appropriated, repixelated. . .

What is a fantasy of catastrophe like? It keeps you wakeful and curious.
and the poet said, "Mighty magic is a number."
another poet asked, echoing another,
"And what *is* your end-cause, what *is* your *desire*?"

truth of the *mystai*

reports that at Eleusis the hierophant
displayed a mown ear of grain
turned to the *pare eidolon*
making a concrete thing

as soon as we realize we own nothing
it's poetry

And if I said
"Aurignacian"
would you
understand?

A woman
but with upper
part bison

Yes, yes you say
a trapdoor
to the animal
you need
looking back

Relief,
hunter's bounty
or odd accompaniment

Otherwise lonely
hybrid obsolete
compression

And if I said
and the brain?
would you understand?

Kiss me here

an upper lobe

How
    born together
a rapturous
gesture toward
animalized . . .

infinity?

No

                    eye turns toward imaginary

I looked over Jordan and what did I see
Drones over Jordan coming after me
Singing the crimes of man
I've got those Anthropocene
Anthropocene blues

Looked into the crystal ball
What did I see
Ghosts of the extincted ones coming after me
A heap of trouble
Coming—coming
Coming after me

Looked in the crystal ball and what did I see
Cadres of humans talking to the streets
Cadres of humans
Changing the frequency

Waking up to the Anthropocene,
Anthropocene blues

a bed of tears
angel of a new place
no fireworks tonight light the town
what ticks? catastrophe
be such a reader of all that goes visionary
outside
walk the same street
stop by the same creek
wash eyes in bright water
water becomes scarcer
world could dry up on social media
but write it differently
lustration rhythm to understand: the end

Does one see fear in Jeff Sessions's eyes
    & that aggrandizing sick smile which is a
 predatory gesture
      of the face, jaw, mouth related to atavism . . . ?
 "I did not declare it so," he said in answer to a question by
Representative Karen Bass of the Black Caucus about Black Lives Matter
Did you see this?
What is the modus operandi of Jeff Sessions, of Alabama?
ICE: whose ads resemble ISIS ads, e.g. "We're coming for you,"
    "We are coming to kill you." Who designs these ads?
Why do we borrow this strategy from our perceived enemy?

If you said thunder, if you said a vital point if you said my *charms never
overthrown*, if you said an instance of an ardent rapture, if you held the
machine yourself in this "handheld" way, as ancient troubadour catching
the figure of woman, as if in spoken song, would be listening. Dwelling
in an illusion of flicker by flicker obdurate language. Chemical code of
the chromosomes. Against interpretation.

So far, a symbiosis. Attest to that. To come to a poetics full blown
under a school desk, taking shelter from fear of nuclear blast & fallout.

Remember how one clutched corrosive-resistant metal dog tag of name & station & identity. Air raids. *In the mind of the child are all times contemporaneous?* It hangs on a ball-chain under your sweater, remember its initial coolness against the skin . . . you are now, someone said, inducted into the paranoid armies of the U.S. of A. In the Vietnam War soldiers put rubber silencers on their dog tags so the enemy wouldn't hear their sound (they wore two tags—if killed one would rest with the body to the grave).

What is a fantasy of catastrophe like? It keeps you wakeful and curious. A disjunct here, cognitive dissonance for someone so young.

What myth is structuring my imagination? The end of democracy?

Playing with war trinkets at home, lieutenant father's spoils of WWII were safe in a strongbox. Some particular ones, medals embossed with insignia, enameled, plucked from the enemy dead. Giving rank and posture, somehow stiff, formal and a gesture from the State which orchestrated the apparatus of Nazidom.

Presumably your child corpse would be identifiable with its metal tag after a nuclear blast. Survive like the gold cavities extracted from victims in concentration camps. But this was not the way to inhabit a body, the child thought. . . . *This is crazy, what dog tag would survive a nuclear blast?* First question for the State.

Men = War. Apparatus is a tough assignment. Can't read you. You are either in or off the mark. Above or below the mark. It is a nonhuman agency: apparatus. A nonhuman gesture is an apparatus. She wanted to soldier to embrace apparatus or so she thought but others who saw differently might convince you of a different approach. Look there a sunset. Look there a catastrophe.

A different approach. At the child's birth, there were miracles. War ending. And there would be some hope for an other who would enter a world beyond apparatus. An arbitrary program is an apparatus. How dull! But she could be a miracle. Hopes pinned to the uniform. Second question for the state. How did it feel to vote in 1920 CE?

—What is a desire to enter a path like soldiering feel like?

—Not arbitrary.

—Necessity is at the gate. *Est-ce que ça te soucie?*

All the "itys" come charging in.

There is a condition not unlike Paleolithic for opportunity. Opportunity comes knocking. In the shape of a woman or holocaust.

Beyond automatic. Because an apparatus obeys a system.

She dreamed about some ingenious objects after she went out, soft weaponry, after she traveled on all those vehicles, after she went out, knobs & button & triggers, wires & dynamite after she joined up because remember she was now not merely out, but "once, out" and it was time to sleep, dream, get up at dawn, and inhabit new battle's ground. Not go down in tragedy.

O Muse
Melpomene,
* by*
your
will
bind
the
* laurel.*

& bring
a bouquet
a calendar round
to mark year's
acclamatio adversa
we
sing
but the light
cease,
congressional men
go rounding
out a hell,
Hill or House
step up, elegy
what
motivation
drive tenebrosity
nuclear free
them?
into fire,
magic's
protozoa
a rip or
tear of Ixchel
choose fuel or
love's
intensity
every divine apo-
phatic wrong
what we don't have
to ring, amuse
negative time's nexus
trick o' fate

come melodious one,
        mother of sirens
        success not be
in sessions of
        patriarchy's charge
shocked from the page
        into mock
crown *vir triumphalis* . . .
it's
 over

streets of the world

All writing decides a galaxy all writing resounds planispheric history. Star stars or stars stars astound. Not be victim to satisfy appetite. All writing is in fact cut-ups history will decide Rimbaud your heat of the world. Role model to cut *voyelles* every Rimbaud's mother's nightmare. To rise up outcry inside supply side. Get crackling on an earpiece oligarchies of the world, slice woes of women. A long delineation. Longer than world be counting. This a whisper, enough of whisper to rise up rise up and wiser, streets of the world. Commission overheard a spin a terrain a soldiering one. She wanted to soldier outta here. She wanted what streets of the world to spin rubric's yes yes commerce, no, a no, no. Tanks of the blown-off world. Earth and rising, beauties of the world. Cyborg offshore a caw caw of major spills and elsewhere no, no, better invite the Amazons in. Cut the dialect the binary the dear word so precious and forbidden, dear futurist. Dear stone. They use the machines to take the streets out of "the out of" streets of the world. Horizon headwater cut cut the cable my beignets my appetite "poor politics, poor pols." Reconstitute polis ban exclusion of women, O women of the world. Metonymic of entire edifice. Waters of the corpse world in media cut lines manipulate desire and show the word don't detonate anyway. "She" assassin Hassan-i Sabbah production in Classic Maya. Textile's Hesiod: they descend from Pandora. Or Rex Tillerson a hex tiller's son, tilling the field a cultivation of one. Angora, of shreds, a mythically shredded world, bleats the world. Tools in the lab make women open tomb and allies slither out. Where voices tremble trouble sleep, there's weeping of the world. He won't accompany poetry when I use the word "resist." Test a roan. Is where Rimbaud was going with order could live systematic derangement of the casino scene, cut cut in with drone lullaby hallucination: seeing that street fights reanimate the world. And Merkel poor Merkel our nuclear safe future to fight fight "poor politics, poor pols." Our man in rendition caged and cut cut the torture O Iran streets of the world arise to cut back forms else mammals suffer. Show tablets a Paleolithic grab all streets the world. Twilight fields of discontent all streets that shadow governments rise up to reason the world. Wounded galaxies feminine discontent insists. "Hear you, people of the word."

What room the ghostlier golden light we reach to. Lines & demarcations. Assume worst has happened deporting undesirables, his French side gypsy purge. Subject to strategy poor poor pols. Its link its drill its despots, murderers in the lurch. Jade rabbit pounding herbs for immortals. Rides up alien virus moon. Magnetize worlds let them course light in unsettled streets of Dreamers, let them go free from cruelty. My William my difficult Burroughs, when in feminine you scold past test me. Burrow in. A guy's in. Goddamn interior ministry of fisheries and assume the worst in writing EPA cuts her exterior of life the glib industry. Selves behind tyrants shelve desire. My loaves & fishes in deep deep water. Foxes' henhouse in hurt and ready. Hexes in the rock house. A steep bantum horror. Roster of silent squawk our jar red to crush. Bleak & white. Streets of the biblio-tech world. Axis of sky. Come down mounds my no, my hacking Russia. Is at some point classical prose, my no, Bulgaria no Romania my Haiti my Egypt, and Poland to come to this coastline America. Ruptured pipelines to caw caw Gulf Stream is seated cut cut to other syndrome fields ripple effect and your domino will fall. Aurignacian, your achtung will fall. Geronimo a domino falls. One percent down. Bombs all fall down, dimensions your strategy. Will history decide "caw caw caw"? Will Iraq? Will Yemen? How many tarots discoveries sound to kinesthetic gulf of arcana everyone. She wanted to soldier a China gulf to anyone. She wants to soldier out of long delineation stars longer than would be counting. Star stars or stars stars. Cut through leak of revolution the occupied future will come out. A page of written words no advantage to leak from nuclear gender. Let the mice in. Circumpolar water denizens unruly genes will come out. Then cut cut the variation images shift to pool sense advantage in processing sound sight cut cut sound to "arise." Of memories stars have been made by accidents. See how calm politics will become. Sperm count down. Non white wonder world. The "walking marriage" of the matrilinear: the China, the India, the Africa. Push a boundary. Pry open pray open let the women out. Woman up! Take all, mandarin widows. Oral consciousness of stars.

radio play: face-down-girl

Men like women who write. Even though they don't say so. A writer is a foreign country.

—Marguerite Duras

narrations for ten virgins:

The kid heads her to an island. Priests & statuary. Pearls for sale. Steps on the agate path. What is your number? It's remote. Thirsting. Remote and a twist. Hands forward. Pretend you want it. Demand you want it. Eros in the child. Voice in the throat. Full-throated. No, better than that. Ease. Distanced. No. Distill. Differentiate. Put a dash in. Tryst as we wait. As if enclosed, Duras. You wrote in a realm all you say. Books of constrained understatement. React. Look up. Cloud is mother and cloister. Imagine no better than that. Years to tell. Who is with you? Alive in gene pool. Makes reckoning easy. Impossible. Day after and fewer persons. Die alone. In a system. Bit the hand in Orientalism. In shade. Don't think and then you stick an old prick into your heart. Orders from the consumer world interpret destruction. He disarms all the parts of you you will use back at him. Parts of a continent. We were in Rabat. She was acting strange in the *riad*. Four bottles of black market wine. Wanted to go back. Job like a teacher's, a guide. Wartime just a kid. Then it was Halong Bay next: her floating world.

Stop to trouble yourself. Life inside the Androgyne Café. Fourteen years old. Life outside, woe inside. It's nighttime when dream is raw. Inhabit the mud lotus. Surveillance. The women loved him your lover his cold power. Wish an outfitting. Visit tomorrow. Tough nerve but comes with a car. He picks you up as girlchild. Makes you a writer. Strap it on in requiem. Raise up the death bier. Help memory. It happened. Intuition by and by. Toward outside. Outward. Virgin in an artist. Wait to rise. End. Of many wait to rise. Roots up. Urge to circle round. Years. First time. If be called writer be called to this. Bliss been standing. Blessed stage of waiting, waiting round. Will remember well. But first put here. Come light a lip. Tight. Lip tight. Lists right. Down to swamp. Not that one where the bad one lives. What imbibes. Earth angels with tiny breasts. Milliseconds. Alights eyelash. Invite motion. Circle round. Urge to circle round. Boats. Future bogs without us. Face on. How do you tell this story so that it haunts forever? Transgression. Order of being. Sorry of waiting, analogue. Will be living. Distill. Then go. Where? Shade. In not. This. All on top of each other being thirsty. First trip to Zen I hit a wall. Recent fires in the hills. Say in French. Lips on Indochine. *Prendre feu. Jouer avec le feu. Avoir le feu sacré. Alcools.*

Are you boy? Could be. Voice from inside. Alone as a writer with bigger reservoir. The cloister binge. If you distill. Drought makes water push further. Oil in the pump room. Extraneous. Think: "It's only a machine." Extraneous. Machination. Wipe down welcome. OK, a border. People wait in line for food. Maybe shelter. Remote chance. People come? Inculcate. Fun up. Sway. However, go, go with Heaven. What, still lives here? Stare. Look out. Four staring phases. Stay with me. Heavens, yes. Looking down. Leaving Beirut. Army brat. Sleep crust. First next incursion. Mirror helps? Moves more remote. Party giver said, "Come to the party with your face on." And, "All the faces will be here." Beneficent. Could dance. Body on. See me. Light-years. There's a silver border. Sayaxché on the Rio Passa. Pottery. Feathers. Contraband. Mahogany. Disappearance. Tell me. Attack? Hear it? The party lights. Did scream. Can you cook can you forage? Some are couples. We take one home. "They've been on quite a jaunt down here quite a time," kid says. Inoculated against colonialism.

I did show her room at the edge of a forest. Placed the checkpoint into further inter-power chambers. Need a password, a new chip. Seed syllable parity circulates. In, out. There's a small relic I'm staring at, small stone Madonna. Fresh and salt. Mix of. Salt save. Just a go. Salt in the mouth. Estuary not swamp. No entrance. Exit for your own risk. Face recognized. I liked the slowness of her sexual speed. Stoic's in a downturn. Motors look like stuffed owls. Ready to move. A stalk holds. Memory at evening. All covered with monkeys. No way to jump out. Bobs up. Shock of animal. Dr. Susan in the jungle with pharmaceuticals, a day with clouds. All a go. Cooking up some bitches' brew. Anticipation of thunder. Will come. Fierce lightning. A tangle. Tough. Science. Ears aquiver for you, listen for rain. Tarp on the heart. Don't let them see you. She was flung in the headwaters. Get a grip on this galaxy. "Gunrunning isn't a hobby down here, you know. Show them how the girls do it when it comes to global warming." *The house a woman creates is utopia.*

Why not. Intelligent eyes on justice. Collection's face. Is collection a face? What matters now. Selected to call this down. Can't see. The blind crocodile. When party mover left says come with your face. She said, a face goes back all the way. You figure what a client state requires. Face alone way back. Similar news. Remember. No wind. Bent down. Bent over. Possible rain. Safe in weather. A pod as explanation. Under our gaze. Peas in a pod. Not remote. Not so everyone. Hey look down. The nematodes. You are trouble. Sorry for the edible crustacean. Peninsula with swallows. Eyelash. Very faint. Moth lash before us. When they make locks. Remote tectonics. Wait. Posture telling. "Put your legs together, girl!" Gene pool extends. System? Realize interference. Lips seal. Operations. Leaf bed. Roots. More remote. Freedom of tides. Face of stowaway all over the news. Bestial behind apparatus, colder cellular childhood. Some plastic surgery he was different, more gregarious but eyes the same: old hipster eyes. He asks me to dance. On the lamb it's called, he wants me to stay with him. Hide behind a woman. They stole our Inca beads at customs. Tentacular: have a wide reach.

Information. Dialing home. Jail restless behind glass communication chamber. Below a border. Shangri-la. Many sections blackened. Ever glad of all action. Without agitation. Tie to Polaris and go to jail. Jupiter next to moon. Own peninsula. Please be there. First, existence, then obligation. Get lines. Night lie down. Head down. Roots walk. That's interesting. Bed of roots. Bedroot. Also, kind old coca love. De facto. Don't notice. Worse for wear in the opium den. Wonder and may. Long to seen. First, incursion. Then move. Sealed. Remote and owned. Shade back. Someone dancing. He got his looks on the lamb. Reckons easy. More indigenous to here. Put down "Zilla"; she gives you the ID. Write it down over the border to Mexico. Over to other. Stir back. Rabbit offers herself to Quetzalcoatl. Ride my moon. Head up. Scratchy record the old Victrola. What's she to you? Slipped the letter in she took a year writing. Got her strange identity back. Between poles. *The great equatorial Source from the North of the earth, says the little white rabbit.* Duras measures endurance. Pokes your gut, underage lover.

Trying to write but dark in here in the prose place. Head down. May be. In the dark book. Aromas released, body alembic in delicate night. From body then cypress. Ginger, frankincense. Lavender. In that order. Of scent. Imagine the cast of characters and their animals. Waiting. Released. Restored. The break. Don't like fracking. The pressure. Then far up. A neck. Break. Pressure. Spine. Go back. Up then. What then? Turn over. Reimagined in prone place. Alembic her laboratory. Couples. Two by two. Stable place. What then? Hands free? Maybe. Back of the mind. Woes of world. Sit face-to-face. Root in another. Knows this. Lie down with me. Hands free. Out of dark, unbowed. Unmask. Stare into the night sky. Space is silent. Didn't I ask to be touched yet? Stare into fire pit along time. Want it. Bring intimation. Trick her in her matrix. Double helix snake of mind. Swathed in death shroud. How make love in internment? Staring into the fire, world flashes by. And all the noise below. An arrangement of some kind, smuggling: aphrodisiacs, contraband, guns. The kid out back, back of the prayer circle, skinny kid, mounting the zodiac.

Across the rice paddy sweet breeze. Darker with a mask on. He'd be an aroma. No bother. May be dark aroma can't see it. She puts boy to bed. Frankincense for everything. Can't see it. The volcano behind rain. Breathe. Tell me to breathe. I may be small. Under pressure. It blisters at the top. No bother. Blisters then steamy at the top. Ooze. What blocks the run? Not so remote. One came. And with one came one. Wait. Earth stand still. Fine reticulation. This is down for us. One & one. This is for "calm." This is "energy." This is "mediation." This is "meltdown." Go up. Turn dried aroma to use. Wondrous body. Future in this. How long? Radio waves. Hear when I go. Source: outer. From us. Truck of immigrants over the border, I wave. Far up. Reimagined. See? Make way. Cenozoic. Make way up. Plume's smoke. Lava. Like a dream. Wait until intermission. Off the counter. Insidious control. But you can get off the floor now. You'll arrive at the airport with concern. When they ask about your extra baggage, say "Kinesthesia."

Put in charge of winning wars. Marrying for the green card. There were some stories. Pretending to love. Surveillance at every turn. Off the table. Intermezzo. Couple forward. You split. Couple to forward. Stares. Ashes block the sun. Words ring. In his day come forward. Not to wait. The lover picking her up around the corner from the school yard. The empires still powerful there though the dreams be scarce. Rotation. Through the small vials. Of vine. Cypress is for wits. Lavender is for everything. Safe in rotation. Wheel of oil. Until parting over stones. Oils from the first incursion. Then moving. Ever and her glade. Not undiagnostic. Put down. When they made the locks I was small. In a posture was erotic. In a small posture. Posture tells a map. Worn down but welcome. Stage with me on the platforms. Prone bodies. Brash incursion of the company. Our country back home is pornographic. Comes from whim. Voice within. You need it more than ever. Losing obstinate virginity. And counting. Colonizers. And counting. How many numbers in our camp of survival. All to offer. Brash. Anticipation is thunder. Scents. Pretend the simian. Likes a nap. It was your own identity you owned in identity. How's that? And they all kept coming on. Mother backstage at the performance: *Blood Wedding*. Someone in the loge you don't recognize.

Stoic in writer downturn, wry smile. Controlling the rhetoric of women's liberation. Inside. Hand under the mount. Discordia. Goddess of strange. Look down. Mud you are. Don't violate. The move made. You tick. Come with you. We meet in alleyway. Escape. The same impasse. Back to youth. Under your skin. Where we begin. Come light up. A line. Mercy is many. Full-throated. Remote. Thirsty. Hands forward. Double helix. Held me. A snake in you. Are you? You come to me as man in a woman's body. Gender jester. Hermeneutics. To tell. Contrive. Up the cudgel. To trick. Roots come up. Out of nothing. Flesh of finger wag at you. Enter. Nerve fields. Cosmic back at you. Barks. Strike. Keeper of secrets. Disoriented. Disgorge. Distant. Discern. Disarm. Diseur. Desire. Disperse. Disclimax. Disseminate. Dissuade. Destroy. Duress. Then saw her. Saw her original body. Someone died for this to hold memory. When? When I went down.

[Constraints were to be as a child, and I had to bring in the son and I had to bring in the mother. I had to bring in the places traveled. I needed to follow the assignment of flowing through virginity & violation. I had to include Marguerite Duras. I had to mention a coven of objects (mirror, feathers, pharmaceuticals, Inca beads) and include earth, air, fire, water. I had to think orally and include one hallucination and mention of one religion: Zen. There could be sounds of a jungle.]

mash butler

Pleasures do not emanate
from the biological body
Crush on you
at present time
That which the thing
is in fact fitting to liken
to the father's
ambivalence
XX chromosomes
perform this accomplishment
Stylized repetition
are you genitally organized?
Is no thing here
variety of form?
Reproducing?
And is ontology?
Is *Timaeus*?
And haunting?
Let's return to
the ancients
Is routed
Where is race
Where is class?
        Woman, a trap
A fool's coat
A beau's voyeur
Seize you
No Christ saver
But
No one butts her
Not irrigating the system
A witty wigged one
Hermaphrodite combine

Not a mother but
like a mother
Not a *chora*
but like a *chora*
Semiotic
Persistence like Irigaray
not Irigaray
but Irigaray
Not Kristeva
but like Kristeva
Rival
feminist sees you
ontology
That mater has a feminine
gender
to be exploded
isn't easy
it can't wait
isn't cause
it can't can't wait
a nucleocentric assumption
lips speak together

Isn't, isn't it not
but a system which
body is assumed
to require maternity

& law of itself
hetero
norma
tivity

Mimicry
      no way . . .

I was born but . . .
nothing perfect
sexed body
not a given

And then
    just sayin'

strangling me with your lasso of stars

(Aimé Césaire)

Night, the immigrant

words were totems
words were spells
were beasts

day slowing down
against a mode of survival

stars are oscillating
stars are fields
waves of probability

words are mistakes
are pleas
ask favors

stuff of Max Planck's constant
probable chronography

stuff of reason
floods & famine
strafing

ache of the day
culture of helicopter
haunted
sound is a menace

take the light
stop the search?
aimless, don't make trouble

obstacles stab of reason
no language you understand
arable? telepathic?

what is authority?
tiny fragile human
authority pitted
against tiny fragile human
pity fragile human

the words were ambiguous
words were closures
words wore a necklace
a lasso, rope, trap

link zones,
represent a field of meanings
animal in my future
conclusion is a starship
matrix of escape

you would reckon a pitch
not a meaning
whirr a world

reckon a sonata, señora
you would never sleep
copter's blues

never sleep
and razor wire

hiding as a specter
what is it?
your woman shadow,
a knife

swords were clipped
words were missing
words are knives

(know another language)

then water
then drowning
then drowned child

the words were continuity
guns & keys
clay, rope, & cages

the man with these things never
stops
hounding

a refugee, a spectator
come to Balzac's Paris
or fourth dimension, Robespierre

come to skyscrapers
stack up here
then disappear

the words were ruses
never let you sleep
they have your number
"coming to get you"

a detonating device
sits below on Twenty-Seventh Street
FBI
a robot detonates a box at 3:00 a.m.

amber alert
stay away from windows
shattering glass
perpetrator on loose

you can live vertically
and create sound
false cybernetics
a world after Darwin

you can hide
you can blend in,
keeper of herds
in trap of appetite

yearning
cavalry at riverbanks
detonating devices
a flaneur

you can never live
the high-pitched urbanity
fever & money
among strangers some shelter
nights on the street

the words were trying
trying to be sanctuary
hide again, telling you
words are victims
"coming to get you"

the Scandinavians open
to close down
hunker down
everyone is a dossier

the stars are projections
shelter is postcultural
come up from South
come up this way
a better life

a leader was opening
then all shut down

a new dream
beyond borders
no expectations
take you in

inner writing
drives an old woman at twilight

words design pursuit
welcome their collapse
then twilight it's slippery
then night again

may art never be forbidden
may all escape their tormentors
words are slippery

crossing to safety
waiting in front of you, night again
waiting,
a bomb in your closet

to identify what is wild
your own ethnography
lend your identity

canoe, a risk
fetishized hunger
take you away

words are citizens
words are enemies
as one writes to reveal them
a map fails

penchant for motive
intense light greets you
out of nothing
migrant celebrity

you might die
stars to guide you
a place to die
to reminiscence

you might be embraced
you might have to run
under a gun

play with dice
another woman at twilight
and another

weird sisters
sound like crows

look up
abstract stars
more pitiless
don't notice you

words are pushing
and break hard

and break hard

and break hard

words could be travelers
could be gentler

and their sound

[When was the Federal Reserve created, and by whom?/ Who was second in command to Jefferson Davis and considered the brains of the Confederacy?/ What was the primary material factor in British sea domination?/ What was Ezra Pound right about?/ How many things don't make sense about the Bering Straits theory of migration?/ What might that mean?/ What was Black Friday?/ What was the Cat & Mouse Act?/ Who funded the Confederacy and why?/ Do you think people employed by the US government are capable of creating al-Qaeda?/ What does the term "false flag" mean? Where was Suha Bishara imprisoned?/ Why was she imprisoned?/Who is Suha Bishara?/ Who kidnapped Mordechai Vanunu?/ Where did this happen?/ Who is Mordechai Vanunu?/ Where was he born?/ Why do race and gender now seem so high on the US agenda?/ What does an eye for an eye and a tooth for a tooth actually mean?/ What is the origin of this formula?/ What are we talking about?/ What is the B.I.E. movement?/ And who invented it?/ Who were the Silent Sentinels?/ What was Gertrude Stein wrong about?/ How many immigrants are in US detention centers on any given day?/ What are "plutonium pits"?/ What are "jellyfish babies"?]

tresses

write this down or the past may forget its part in the current, Akilah said

1.

brutalize   origin   organza
"spurned as a feminist"
so we think so we march on
Sojourner Truth sold
with a flock of sheep
for one hundred dollars
"Ain't I a Woman?"
horrific time ago
be slave,
abolitionist
was like to think
rustling the assemblages
one such a body might offer
as one does these parts
and feminists needing people
colors cling to
as they do: "outed"
was like to think
artist spirit
complicated colors
of many patched skins
and migratory bodies
through channels of
ambiguity
and wounds no matter
and synthesis *is* matter
to a feminist
syncretic form turns

singer into spirit-griot
offers you flowers
parched of atmosphere and
more tough-wound-resilience,
sisters & ghosts
of the paper parted and
radicalized
to mold it
and laugh
the forest made
the monkey
the forest made three crows
but the cave & steppe,
make the human sister
bejeweled, tattooed,
or wrapped
with capes & shrouds
(and you feel) the world
in vein
how it wants to
bloodlet
remembers
masculine
tone as it might be
historically trauma
that they earn it, the guys
try us on again
for sighs,
as we sit and stitch
with prudence "her" story
a kind of wild stamina
a ubiquitous valorous
body summons
in the drawing
in the cloth

on the foolscap page
in the paint
snatched up by handmaiden
and in a case
of metallurgy
become instrument
of daughters
"what methods of political
thought can poetry
uniquely perform?"
munificent
hand-painted
caves & caskets
and in each
a kind of *pietà*
of ubiquitous ones
who carry
ancestor's thread, DNA
made of papier-mâché
artist's one-on-one
dreamer, double, familiar
phantom in a dream
and these ideas
vanish from our sweet
world
explicitly against tyranny
enactment of haunted
"witness" faces
*(have you seen the other side
and what does it look like?)*
then a maritime
floating puppet walking in
another century's steppes
over this
civic wide hospitable Brooklyn

(eighteenth century
how long our suffragette cause?)
took a species of
troglodytes to the perimeter
spun gauze around species
cocoon-protection . . .
nurture it
to walk inside a tome
a tomb a shadow box
to make law
that put so close a mark
on life
as to be furred, feathered,
dazzled
embroidered
the purr ended in there
never "did not want to go no further"
the life cycle of woman
Sojourner spoke Dutch until
age nine
stopped at a
laboratory of sleeves
O sisters
Jun'ichiro Tanizaki
describes the
head & hands only
of the Bunraku woman
recess shadows
stick-pole woman
syntax derived
that she be vertical
and frozen inside flesh
teeth blackened or perhaps
with green lipstick the better
to glisten

in lantern-locked light
(never again)

2.

triple consciousness
is a braid in consciousness
out of a tomb
hunger is food is a chorus is a query
where that god be at is a bridge is transgression
is a trace is a valley is what's allowed
what's forbidden
not name but girl-writing speaks
for now she is come to the warm time
speaks a name in tresses
this is a *trestle of hair.*
carries   supports
covers ground she said
clap and so she did. clap.
as in performance.
twist of an appropriation
for the *white slave bitch* who speaks another name
she says she says
"leave that body right here to be sucked"
in the valley unharmed
yea yea twist of the air
all the characters in the fairy tales
will not hold back desire behind eyes. but
rupture for writing
for girls who seek a double name
in a valley that is a soul place.
clap. as in this performance
that writes its way out to *refashion the tongue.*
American.

tress that is a stress. that is a span for this
new naming. Gk *trikhi*, rope, from *thrix, trikh*—hair
what is the racial gain
what is the terminology
of relationship in a white tee
or fairy tales with animals in them
what is a base desire what is a performance?
clap, she says. *in a Polaroid picture frame.* snap.
the hair between the legs. girlword.
"tressels" she said.
how do they feel what is not permissible to feel
and that is the tress that is a trestle
is the vessel is crux to cross this girl
in writing of first desire
and cross that barrier for desire.
trestles. that makes a way like girlword
like a triple conscious word-world, a frame
that stops mind in a matrix of mortality working
in a language necessary to voice alive alive
o: *trestles of hair.*

patriarchus

detour of a clinamen

—*Jacques Derrida*

drone & cope? **did** trap culture ruinously triage **did** chaos
reshape history girls in the dark trying to read a man's world
free electron with atom collides then enfolds **didn't** grok tangent
patria to make kinder spread dissing widening then worsening word-lore
did assassin's teeth *patriarchus* tectonics tethered pathological oligarchy
did memory bites surrounds money **did** this a grammar digital
language entwined polis vernacular holds **does** this **does** this
curses tightening coil antic of animal on kill irreparable
marked **did** this enslave "get lost" **does** this spits out derivatives
did this out of nothing: *anamnesis* out of *lethargon* un-forgetting
fields of unsheathed wheat cots bunk prisons inside are cussed **did** this
conditions apocalyptic scenarios laws to ensnare agency! agency!
grind & toil of meat wheel how dallied this world gone mute you **did** this
in oscillation **does** this a coup all turns **did** this stressed this world
crude in light iron fist photon disquiet waves of probability *Gematria*
code to names & words **am** diamond fortress **am** forest of refugees
rescue men & boys **am** escape falling city poets with cusp on zodiac **did** this
projectiles continuum *I feel love I feel love* and *gnosis* **am** your spy agency
hacking & cyber warfare "Winterlight" "Fox Acid" servers
impersonated as person **am** legitimate imposter topos woman
politic proletarian linked in profile not happy in melancholia
identity page be tracking gems quotients situate the frame **did** this
transcendent *philosophia perennis* theater of dreams **never** give up
never forget you sold us out "sold us down the river" **did** this in cheap coinage
slaver's tongue "bank's closed" "goosed outta here" "shrank us"
"greased us over" lifetimes will remember you **did** this you **do** this
will be pacifying will be enriching will be magnetizing will be destroying
and never wear out a cosmic war on you
my name is anne waldman and I approve this message

trickster feminism

I'm a scout on the quiet road into it.

—Leslie Scalapino

Always post-post never-never's or always bold holocaust road maps, one or the other guiding one through future mine fields; quick answer, the coyote and trickster . . .

—kari edwards

Called back by the vicissitude of current attacks on LGBTQ communities, institutional misogyny, ICE raids on undocumented immigrants, saber rattling with North Korea, psycho-massacres, blindsiding bargain with Iran, upped ante on racism, Anthropocene weather complexities, destruction of infrastructure, and rising homelessness and forced migration. Undoing any compassionate gestures a civil servant might as leader muster, where are we? Exposed. And scrying into a stranger future. Collusion. Impeachment. All to come. But the fix is in. Protocol of the controllers' last bastion of white male rule exposed. Dead-end coup. You have to cut ignorance at its root, no compromise. This is it. I'll be the perfect witch for you. Cotton Mather no longer at the controls. Bishop Landa in meltdown. "If the weather don't get us, the supremacists will." Outsperm their bank accounts. Voodoo abetted by science. Tantric rites to cut the aortas of the perverters of enlightened mind! Laugh through tears. Long nights under siege waiting for the levees to break and you make a model of repair for unborn genius Bodhisattvas coming after. Trying to remember role in late capital poet-life-vow-archive, a feminine principle, whatever gender. Outrider scholar & philosopher Paul B. Preciado (formerly Beatriz Preciado; born in Spain, 1970; transitioned in 2015) has prescient analysis in Testo Junkie, *a book of radical textual experimentation, often compared to the work of William S. Burroughs. Preciado talks about how we are living in a punk-cyber-gothic Middle Ages of the bio-information empire. We are swimming in nuclear semen in which we are learning to breathe like mutant beasts. Some—in his view—think that contemporary civilization has substituted an industrial or ergot-like foundation for onto-theology. But nothing explains the present functioning of our societies. The contemporary techno-porno-punk empire relies on new slogans: "Consume* and die." "Have an orgasm and make war." And to paraphrase: don't forget to continue to consume and to come after your death. This is the thanato-pornographic foundation of the new empire. Our presence to ourselves as a species, Preciado continues, could be described today as "prosthetico-comatose." "We've closed our eyes, but we continue to see by means of an array of technologies, political implants that we call life, culture, civilization. It is, however, only through the strategic reappropriation of these biotechnological apparatuses that it is possible to reinvent resistance, to risk revolution." Preciado invokes a new porno-punk philosophy as we wait to morph, change planets. And revolt! "Let us be worthy of our own fall" is the rallying cry.

scry into crystal

the hours we pass are *horae*, are stars
smoothed chalcedony,
stick bundles of quill pens
   glint
write into
only poetry
history of mind
  all you do
or say record
only poetry
hematite or vermilion rubbed into
incised lines of shell texts
so they shine in poetry
valuable is the
ivory-like bone of manatee
sought after in Bishop Landa's day
harpooned in tidal creeks
shallow waters
conquistadores
descend
shimmery from purpose
ear to

wicked heart, a metronome

you have to assume touch
sexual, heat of it
simultaneity
dimensions all times
no two-ways about it
a black hole right next to you
be careful
you fall in love
alert with conch alarum
water-lily jaguar to
help in crepuscular power
we don't push buttons here
we cross the lei lines of desire
& transformation
no, to be out on the road
with false chief-many-cars
hide from eclipse, lovers
protection from perils

hurricanes,
floods, & catastrophe

closely curtained sedan chairs
limited to gardens

if a woman assaults her husband
she will perform
slave labor
for one year
suicide to show
gratitude when he dies

limited to gardens

gather all supplies you can muster
seeds for better survival options
and water jugs
bring in a bubbling brook of imagination
to stay thirst
and blankets
you will want a shortwave radio
take the pop cans you buried in the yard just for this
your relatives will thank you
what vehicle best for the road?
games are good, if you travel with children
books always and interactive puzzles
skin of sleep
skin for retreat, cloak of darkness
pores closing like flowers past bedtime
may you never die
this is it
be a stream enterer

3.8-billion-year symbiosis
tiny swans perch improbably
on threadlike spirals

noteworthy are the long fingers
traces of red paint
survive on the cheeks
& top of the head—

steatopygous
full legs & buttocks
final Neolithic

married a woman so they could
have poetry contests together

a kind of trobairitz revival
women take back talk back in the voice of women
as if men . . .
surely some want to be men, right?

Confucian etiquette:
reserve
quiet
chastity
orderliness
governing herself to maintain
a sense of shame

she was small and hidden and like the rest
wanted agency in the Linnaeus room
relationship afloat with an Iron Age anchor & algae beneath
make things with love
keep your sense of awe & beauty

human hands at oars
wings encrypted like frescoed angels
crown of glory or baby coming out
after dark machinery we say crowning,
crowning baby coming out!
new baby coming out, new urgency
meet the overpopulated day

the galaxy's disk, the Sagittarius Arm

a tasseled whip
means "riding a
          horse"

three terra-cotta aryballi
in form of helmeted heads
revealed with a griffin

a guise without guile waiting
salubrious seductive one, a stealth missile
bugs off

Elias Cairel, you phony troubadour

and has a word for facial design: *lianpu*
that is an actual event for a broken world . . .
O false elementals
look into diaphanous future feminism

in the Tang dynasty
there
was great demand
for priestesses as sexual teachers
& initiators

you neglect your makeup
it is easier to get a priceless jewel
than to find a man with a true heart

the Taoist priestess arrives in ceremonial robes
and taps your spine as you gaze into the waterfall
a fountain of youth for the next generation
let the opera of Kali Yuga begin

we will have basso profundo
we will have a tenor beat
we will raise the ante on her back
in sounds created from structures
unrelated to breathing

we used to have space bars which benefitted the
typing of the devotees who closed our ranks late into the night

we had pasteurization

we used to have dog tags

we used to have a spacecraft we understood and someone explaining
gravity

scratch my blackboard, please and soon

we used to be gay and getting out of combat and did "not telling"
did not telling not telling not telling not telling

we used to study slower, tight the eye & mind
can't you shake, vibrate, wobble? not tell?

we used to do this on a strange dance floor
do tell

can we be used?

did she breathe fire,
did she walk on fire
did she battle the masculine wits to a pulp
did she overdose on testosterone
did we succumb to mere guise?
or does it matter?
day to day moment to moment
        a struggle
     for
identity,

    all continually a sentence a question of sentience
that coevolved with the orchid bees of Peru
male bees looking for perfume
    brush against my leg . . .

girl child stands by with cornucopia
now jobless or godless
   sweet rain
in a fiction of birds & nights
    generator
on
below
      what is her scent?

the scent of the feminist to be
how old is she now
when will she know
next generation's modus

and what does it offer?
how do you join child to world?
how does she get seeded in you
what propensity to act?

a measure for cornfields
when the mountains pry us apart
   sexual longing for place   no strings . . .

country far away,
how we were handled far away
by *lepidoptera*

one creature or person reflects inside other
   then wild exodus of doves

Miriam of bitter water, rebellion
    Miriam elevated how
nations are as a drop of water
crossing Sea of Reeds
patriarch casting off horse & rider

she is our seer, sister of Moses, of Aaron
     rebel against the pharaoh
the midwives must be spared this bloody task
but down the horse & rider . . .
     enmity in a stagnant land
a small story told around a fire
mir mir mir
Miriam with timbrel, with voice with lineage
her sound, where is her Book of Miriam?
how clear a sound
come all the way through her speaking . . .

mere a bye

or is it?   princess of imagination
Rajasthani

wake up your Andes mistress of the milpa
  as measuring spoons
     calibrate new desire

   liquid season . . . her scent

in love with all scale
 and wings of luminous birds
augury
conjured here, small avian bodies tell future as
          they die

stone stone more conjugal stone

breaks and you feel tug of muscle & bone

what's not said, how many dead

counting, or "disappeared"
    counting as you climb step by step
stone stone stone stone

but when it comes to
open street, festivals, flutes
civic declaration of progress
wave a little flag
genuflect
obligatory show of patriotism

parade snappy blue back home
    and white tees democracy in red crisis

what place
wrapped up on these
inimical altiplano "shores" . . .

quick to flare in her serape
coca leaf against the chill

I thought maybe a photo
I thought cards with falcons on them
chain with tiny gold cross around a neck
falcon standing attentively
on a necklace
I thought again: Peru

and "save a soul"

dream city   reunion of cloud with mountain
or reunion   thoughts like clouds
          cumulus,   cirrus

dream city

violent Picchu   where ice once
crystalizes streets

not this year
not this time
not this century

thinking about sound in this conundrum
      as you chant
"stone stone conjugal stone"

sound de-territorializes
weather   and my colors cling to you in weather

you sang "cumulus," as heap
no it wasn't a heap of cloud
It was "cirrus" I sang,
high above ice crystals
lord it over,   streaks the trail of that airplane

and grows fainter replicas of ourselves little humans
inside its shadow

a curl of cloud wisp
      hair   much like yours
descends over my body in tantric shape

the anthropoid
is grief
as women . . . is, power?

worn

to fierce tenderness in new feminism

I serve her from the left-hand side

I serve her some cockney and serve some pidgin English

I serve her in Bahasa Indonesian

I serve her my hybrid narratives

I serve her succulents on a plastic tray, image of a rotating fowl

I fight the hens-in-a-blanket and the pigs-in-a-blanket incarnations

I fight the rubber tread incarnation

I sing three anthems for old feminism

I leave my bull dyke truck in the driveway, revving

I serve her from the right side and serve her
my red-state hot sauce, my red-state syncretic conglomeration of
philosophies,
my red-state melancholia, red-state pharmacopoeia

I serve all the blues I got

I take off my jaguar swimsuit (eighty degrees in Manhattan)
in front of an array of contradictory intentions

one is seeing the other is invisible in front of my vanity

smooth skin, smooth as your lines

we used to be able to outdo the future

we were never stuck in the past

we always wanted a mystery of narration

not just in a line when you edit

we laughed harder at mistakes & puns

and we always wanted each other, saw you there

saw me here, stole you from there

because we used to be there

and now here, your lines

used to be able to outdo the future

see a syllable
inside body chakra
seed it
O royal robes of the Vedic age,
stay humble
   O Varni

you must be, Lady
Adamantine,

you must be Moving Robe Woman
& Lozen, prophet of the Chiricahua Apache

analytically cool
as you look down on the patriarchs

a supply world they rule with no spiritual cachet

nothing to lose

but everything

deathside with corpse of light
there's a ladder in the body

earth is always magic

you are earth matter

and you are ephemeral too

crossing your voice with silent space

silhouettes on the shade.

rite

working with willow rods that's the method,
bring great bundles of them,
put on the ground scatter them
pronounce them, saying:

"here's one"
"here's another one"
"here's one, there . . . over there . . ."

willow rods, very consoling   we'll clear the ground
you don't have to be a Scythian . . .

and then the ones behaving more like women use a different method

they take a piece of the inner bark of a lime tree
cut it into many pieces
which they keep twisting and untwisting around their fingers as they
make effigies of themselves, willow rods of women saying:

"there's a turn"
"there's a turning"
"there's a rowdy one"
"there's a moist one"

"there's one we lost to negligent wind"
"another one burned up"
"one folded down a sparrow's cheek"
"how many turnings in a twisty one?"

a million, more than you can ever hold
makes the pronouncers happy
surveyors of tractor and sage
and when all goes out

remember eclipse telling you this could all go out
women too? women go out?

but for love & mystery
willows rods, willows rods
you know this, women
to fool the hearts of men

staying up all night, notice the moon and its macabre signal

and hemp vapor tents on the horizon

walk upside down in the footprints of the living

entanglement

In the Dark Times, will there be singing?
Yes, there will be singing, about the Dark Times.

—*Bertolt Brecht (1939)*

Entanglement is my ransom

Entanglement imagines when we shed our skins

Skins keep talking

And shed our sex the sexes keep talking

All the ways to make love
spooky affection at a distance

Entering a chat room with other galaxies
desire & appetite
Where your hand reaches out
worlds of poetry
you don't need description
mind that holds all galaxies of poetry
in deeper listening
or sounds the jazz woman makes

You are represented by those sounds

That's you, singing

Lifting off in libation

Hammurabi's code woke the other one

The two as one, born together

Then separated, women within women recongeal

Perfect dimensions for the spider, the fly

She leaves me split, she is my other, she is my unknown
one of the pair knows what measurement has been performed on the
other   But how?

She abandons me; she never abandons me

Entanglement I think will always sleep with me

Old woman particles

Two forms continue in a landscape miles apart

The bleak and the fecund

We warm as we cool

Worlds collide when tangents weep

The planet got close last night

And we go thirty-one thousand miles per hour to fly by
entanglement, mysterious partner

Physical origins of coupling to the upper atmosphere
by coupling

I saw you singularly, planet lore, plant impermanence coupling

Then we looked to plants, smaller ones, morphed through tundra

Light coming after me from the multiverse

People of distant places with diverse customs will waken

My skin turns in the dream, no longer whiteness

My seventh century looks different from yours

My skin goes down, peels off in the fourth dimension

We are not all winners yet, worn with ragged time

Born and etched with drifts of snow

We cross the summit of Mes Aynak, southeast of Kabul

Fall on our knees to pray

Along the Silk Road, old redemption

Syncretic tumble

We morphed and have compounded ourselves to layers of entanglement

My mother was not a copper mine, my heart was not a sieve

Crumbling ruins of dark mud brick buildings

Bamian valley with its empty niches

Vacant sockets for Buddha

Look inside

The caves of Mes Aynak were used for training by Al-Qaeda for
9/11 highjackers, then abandoned, cool stones

Buddhist remains sent to a copper mine

Archaeologists everywhere struggling in the fractured dream

Scrape the heart

Entanglement is impermanence

Maybe, but wait

A citadel

How much hope in a citadel

Aborted treasure

Distant cousins from Ajanta

My womanly Gautama, entangled tense-lipped one, nested here

Entanglement never rests
But rest now from circumambulation
Om Con Be Gone

Misters all release us
Kin of triumph
What turns uncircling
Chaos is venal

The worst words you could be spat upon by
You'll transcend

Separate body never rests searching itself within language
(speak of love)

Measure consciousness by this poetry, hers, hirs
In name begins debt encoded all sound
spooks a name in mustered awe
trick o' archive's life, the mother

Come carry the sun outside, vibrational ones

See us in new light with old and modernist ancestors
A veil lifts
May all thinkers and mystics abound
A vie to sea and moan

Ever circle around a name
Christine de Pisan
an appeasement
Greek Crown a win her
Mere a bye
Sore wan eye
After been
Um um caliph's tomb

A tongue a tongue

Wall stone craft
Volt a ring declare
Moan's veil from young grave again
Am a lee

Girt intrudes and *les* beings all grounded to this task
Move century a few inches: stein is stone

Lore Rhines the sub alt tress

Mar *rien* moored
An auld linguistic stew

Auld tray lured

Audio loud

Wren a line over brooks

Barb a guest
Not to bury

Dyed Anne deed's prime

Kayacker sure

Loud her back

Ask a verdure

May may bur sin brooch

Hold esteem
Mean alloy
Am car some

Mara boot

Burn a debt
Renew a glad man
Jar knot

Not all lease a knot lease, *onna-bugeisha*

Woe mean

Claw din rank kin

Suit up, feet forward in the maelstrom

Entanglement: plaintive dawn song

Alba, alba, parting poets bid adieu

Missing you, seeing you in a leaf, a shell

Care a lee's knee
Ye wan rein her

Always remote, always inside me
Puzzle of the poem, communicates
Shape-shifts behind trees
May may burst a bruise

Distill and seal measures for entanglement

Longing to be enveloped

I lean miles

Nor bay a sea full up

A word just out of reach where she had been in sentence

Tesserae, the fragments say something about song & vocal cords
about cultural devastation

The caliphate earning millions from the sale of Assyrian artifacts

Bastards of Utopia

Any hope here?

You have to figure it out for yourself

Cool task & sickle lianas

I stopped by the Mutanabbi Market in Baghdad

All the books were in goat, they were in lamb, they were in saffron

Err rick a hunt

All the books were partitioned before and after crisis

Lay deed murmur saw quipu

The books were the key to the investigation of entanglement

Science is hard upon us

Industry is fighting my visionaries

Coal & oil are the enemies of my visionaries

In the Iroquois tradition, seven generations look up from the earth

Entanglement is the complicated mother of all seven

Born together, fall apart, reactivate

Wedded to infinity, it keeps happening

I'll walk there in trickster garb, amulets under clothing, red menses cord
a three-bladed *phurba* of compassion to kill ego,

necklaces of silver skulls, mantra for blue Tara, medicine's Buddha

Visualization: inseparability of action & compassion

When you walk there shed the images you see
And go back in substitution, unfrock, get down

How not become our own volcano?

Visit a ring of fire

Volcanoes were entangled

Act as mirror into my lower atmosphere

Entanglement eschews boundaries

Politics of sonorities

All the organs collapse

I am a dithyramb again

Lie down with the cobra

Tell me ye olde cobra migration narratives

Tell me: collapse of tree and a deluge

Tell me: the claims of the dead on entanglement

Webs, intimate letter of truth & birdsong

Entanglement holds the audience

Entanglement: spellbind phenomena

Be kind to strangers, they are your entanglement

Find our utopic text on the other side of the world

Assignment:
Find our perfect fifth-wave feminism
And think how you would sing about it
To the Kurdish women of Rojava,
To the first person in the world.

trick o' life

Nothing needs doing. I'm idle and free now.

—Yu Hsuan-Chi (c. 844-868)

this is and this is
  and
 this is the way it looks
writing purgatory
and this is and this is
  its sound
   ghost in the syntax
astrology under
    "now" time
not favorable
   hide from eclipse
will you step forward
     have a woman's back?
this is the way it looks
  to be alive in disaster
trick o' life
  crossed
  innumerable
 prescient variables
and this is this is this is
    the way it is
how ancestors
  worshipped sun, ocean
 sky   soil
 illusory world
appearance
 wonder it
on knees?
and can't teach us anything

of global burning
and we forget
    rites to
hold elders inside us
    lest flee, lose track
secrets
    how to think
sing   supplicate
    and fake it too
con of the woman
    gone rudderless,
unaccountable
without precept
this is and this is
  robotics you have
created
    without me
being able to
design an "end effector"
handlike tool at
    end of robot's arm
to caress
 my secret flower
pinch nipple
    cross strait
of flesh
  turbulent
anachronism
    antithesis reality
  crosses a page,
courtship
belly, thigh, ankle's
    lacustrine groove

    this is and this is

fluid like bell keeps
   resonant
     and precarious night
hooks us together,
   inextricably
aspects of identity
        matrix-oppression
intersection of everything
     breathes

sister outsider
   roil in you, in all

treacherous passage
   of corpse light
victims in corpse light
     overlapping yugas of
   demon feminine
jokes, hypnogogic
   assignments
  get back in gear
cook up nothing
   not the good shepherdess
     but body of query
I won't wake
   up with Alexa!

are you ontological
   and haunting?

done with chicanery
  of the tech world
strutting & fetching
   & fetching not your game

for the human?
gone idle? rest on a laurel?

this is crisis
   intervention
and this is how to reckon it
these are modalities
  break down
ever meek, mild
trappings or sonatas
of desperation
what is
   your thousand
        year plan?

hearts trapped in
person-like-things
    artifice
of imposters
this is scripting
  self
awry
this is transitional and
  these are transitory
fake persons
false assassins
rubber dagger
  at heart
weather of salt &
     sand & tears
float a new sound
return the effigy to its cold box
put the dolls away
turn in your armaments

glowing embers,
     last ordeal
barefoot over coals
the practice of dhikr
the Anastenarides
the Rifa'ya
 or tribal songs
     past midnight

why go home?

the *hadra* of Algeria
drums and flutes
"imitate the behavior
& manners of
     the animal exactly"
possession trance
and rhythmic pounding on
one foot

a raucous cry of Allah
   breaks
 from chest
  or other male name meme

and there are those who devour
lions panthers jackals

emboweling and tearing out
their power for themselves

artisans of entry
into trance
     erotics will endure
and inside chaos
     you hallucinate

picture of
    woman-body-at-rest
as musicant

here is harmony now

prophet or augur
as *oikonomia*

telestic   mantic   poetic
        erotic
Jamila in Medina

moved by the memory
    of her homeland

camels hurry to reach camp again

something of mystery
    moves people
    resting
free of gauntlet
    learning songs in
middle of the night

come Ghazalan and Hinda

in *furor poeticus*

toss back
    enemies of life
    ever on toes
but materiality to rest
body in its cone
its sheath

its sleeve
its disguise
undo the havoc of
    death
be ever homeward
    these are mechanisms for
performance
lash against totalitarianism
and people walk free to
  morph to
      outer galaxies...
beyond worlds of dust
aching for new homeland

we are bereaved
  and awakened
abandon
  pirate space?
could one only say it?
saying is action

in the spirit of all
    we can't see
corpuscles
 & new planets
 thoughts are clouds
being human provides for
 being around
an act of
poetry
 tied into language
   and hold
yourself
 within its mellifluous knot

women write parrot poems

embroider phoenix gowns
white jade hairpins flaunt the moon

"we'll never be men"

where's all this beauty heading?
din of confusion
war drums on the street

barbarous things
I had to write
my assassin's dream
had to conjure my last breath
to disappear
within
animation of drum & larynx
I offer crystalline chants
just scribble out poems

Year of the Fire Hen.   Year of Infinite Protest.
        Sarva Mangalam

coda: time to gambol withal?

sell a soul to the devil
security's clearance
praise offerings to hilltops
throw of dice
werewolves, orishas, Papa Legba
meet up after dark
trickster down & dirty
trickster in the nunnery
impudent or oblique
trickster in the binary
let's get trickster
outside the settlement
evolves cavorts hypnotizes
measure of the battle
for transforming
to indigenous time
post-government
it was shadows it was mountains
it was nukes to guide us
assaulting weapons
hatched in trap o' mind
floods and jumping
if it was jumping time was it
the way if peace comes
at end of fight
there is leaping, cheer
piper pipes a song to hear
and you hear it loud & clear
trickster pipe this song to me
how much longer will I be
covert operation
bring us down it was a girl's turn
put on mask or play dead

or inhabit avenger head-set
quasar laughs inside
loop of science speaks
world's negligence as memory
on which existence & truth stand
post-modernity snag
who is hunting
who counts years when
pen comes to hand
when words outlast
the bad guy is moot
say "impala to guide us"
heart in throat
beautiful animals dying on us
a Sybil calls out
words in another tongue
are you there?
& ladder is let down
come up now
climb up to firmament
elusive or decisive when peace
is in the clouds
with all the Immortals
comes into head no gun in sight
shakes like a bell,
recalcitrant body a warning
those who keep nothing secret
could trickster be mercenary?
trickster was memory
was reward
made you wonder about hunger
and then she didn't
trickster was a kind of hunger
you were altered in your lust
you were sheltered

but trickster never lusted
a straight line
quick-fix trickster
in the long term
internment
a day's mist a word as in keep it
inoculated for saner time
if knowledge still grounded
in love is sacred before spectral
what is long since
returned in my book
this must have been a
psychopathic liar time
surveillance time
must have been too few
wanting time to gambol withal
strife slips in sunwise when
you're not looking
did you get a look at her?
queen of retribution, of justice
worried allegorical dimension
does she serve purpose in time
trickster: does she light up in you?
wisecracks float
"don't go cynical on me"
world on suicide watch?
and everything hurts while laughing
recover footing
bail ain't so easy
unwind, they say, no one to frame you
tools in lab, a fool's deal
study the face of mechanical power
all apparitions
hysteria out of public throats
tender post-millennial rage will save

from savage weaponry we pray
precarious tipping point,
no longer sings the nightingale
but still hope a metallic recording
few blocks down
different kind of bird
what I never understood
of "stool pigeon"
dusty road which didn't detonate
breaks away in tones,
a form future remembers
of driverless cars
a lighter rail
when human was a campsite
undesirables turned saints
flurry of carelessness
we'll all be toxic,
coddled in complicity
tell me how in devastation
adventure continues
droning out
for the $ laundering protest,
don't be dazed around criminals
take the wheel of office again
boycott, stomp out,
plead, hold peace for the
ancient anarchist ghost mothers
rocking & fanning themselves
Hecate! Hecate!
endurance in a dream,
invaders of a room bred
of investigation's murky morass
same demons in the belfry
those who cast out
round up

incarcerate break soul of
those who try
unshackle
rules of subservience
but how get supper to homeless
shivering at crossroads
with keening imagination
however jinxed!

NOTES & CITATIONS

Opening epigraph from Lewis Hyde, *Trickster Makes This World* (New York: Farrar, Straus & Giroux, 1998).

Opening epigraph from Jonathan Cott, *The Search for Omm Sety* (New York: Warner Books, 1987).

trick o' death: *"and the alive, like you, ahunted."* Frank O'Hara, "In Memory of My Feelings."

crepuscular: "crepuscular" evolved out of street-writing. I thought of the Force Arcana, the tarot card of strength, as an image for protection during protests on the streets of Manhattan, 2017, against a deck stacked with growing malignancy.

melpomene: *"There had been catastrophe . . . destruction of the world."* Robert Duncan, *The H.D. Book* (Berkeley and Los Angeles: University of California Press, 2011), edited by Michael Boughn and Victor Coleman. Used by permission of Michael Boughn.

melpomene: *"Researchers now working . . . navigating in total darkness."* Christian Caryl, "Predators and Robots at War," *The New York Review of Books*, September 29, 2011, www.nybooks.com/articles/2011/09/29/predators-and-robots-war/.

melpomene: *"O Muse Melpomene, by your will bind the laurel."* Ezra Pound, *The Cantos* (New York: New Directions, 1996).

streets of the world: "streets of the world" inspired by texts in Brion Gysin, *Let the Mice In* (West Glover, VT: Something Else Press, 1973).

strangling me with your lasso of stars: Footnote from "Questions for Citizens" submitted by Anne Waldman to the PoeticCitizenshipToday.mp3 conference, The Graduate Center, CUNY, New York, November 16, 2017. List by Ammiel Alcalay and Anne Waldman.

tresses: Reference to Kiki Smith's "Sojourn," an installation presented by the Sackler Center for Feminist Art, Brooklyn Museum, 2010, and in Part 2 to lines from Akilah Oliver, *The She Said Dialogues: Flesh Memory* (Boulder, CO: Erudite Fangs/ Smokeproof Press, 2009).

trickster feminism: Anohni (formerly Antony, singer and activist) organized a

"Future Feminism" exhibit with events at the Hole on Bowery, New York City, September 2014, in which some of the ideas in the poem "trickster feminism" were generated. An earlier version of the poem was read in the gallery space, an event curated by Kiki Smith.

trickster feminism: Paul B. Preciado (formerly Beatriz Preciado), *Testo Junkie: Sex, Drugs, and Biopolitics in the Pharmacopornographic Era* (New York: Feminist Press, 2013).

trickster feminism: Danielle Dutton for the form of the "I serve" litany, from *SPRAWL* (Los Angeles: Siglio Press, 2010).

entanglement: "entanglement" evolved out of ongoing protest and street-writing, and has had iteration on the album *Untethered* (Fast Speaking Music, 2017) and in recent performances with Meredith Monk.

trick o' life: "trick o' life" appropriated cut-up lines from *Classical Chinese Poetry*, translated and edited by David Hinton (New York: Farrar, Straus & Giroux, 2008). Used by permission of David Hinton.

VISUALS

Cover drawing and lettering design for *Trickster Feminism* by Laurie Anderson. The image is based on a rabbit-headed yogini from the 64 Yogini Lokhari Temple in the Mau subdivision of Banda District in the Bundelkhand region of Uttar Pradesh, tenth century CE. The actual statue has been broken and the upper part of the body resides forty-five miles away at the Garhwa Fort. Sometimes a woman's mind is seen as an obstacle, and yoginis are often depicted with animal heads to magnetize the *siddhi* or supernatural power of these creatures. Yogini temples most likely originated with indigenous Adivasi and others' folk traditions, and were blended with the cults of Shakti and Tantrism.

Image of painting by David Gianonni of Arcane XI La Force from San Tarot, 2017.

Photographs from "Rocky Flats Then and Now: 25 Years After the Raid," an exhibit and conference at the Arvada Center for the Arts and Humanities in Arvada, Colorado, by Maximilian Davies. Performance by the author and Toni Oswald.

Photograph performance with Anne Carson, inside Andy Goldsworthy's Clay House at Glenstone, by Ali Nemerov, 2017.

Anne Waldman has been a prolific and active poet and performer for many years, creating radical new hybrid forms for the long poem, both serial and narrative, as in *Marriage: A Sentence, Structure of the World Compared to a Bubble, Manatee/Humanity,* and *Gossamurmur*, all published by Penguin Books. She is also the author of the magnum opus *The Iovis Trilogy: Colors in the Mechanism of Concealment* (Coffee House Press, 2011), a feminist "cultural intervention" taking on war and patriarchy, which won the PEN Center Literary Award for poetry in 2012. She has been deemed a "countercultural giant" by *Publishers Weekly* for her ethos as a poetic investigator and cultural activist, and in 2015 was presented with a lifetime achievement award from the Before Columbus Foundation. Waldman has always championed the bringing of poetry as well as protest into public space and assembly. She was arrested at Rocky Flats with Allen Ginsberg and Daniel Ellsberg in the 1970s, reading poems that challenged rail deliveries of plutonium for the manufacture of pits for nuclear warheads. She was part of the protests during the Chicago Seven trial and has been involved with agitprop for decades, from early "Street Works" on Wall Street to working with Occupy Art and, most recently, The Federation, PEN America, the New York Public Library, Poetic Justice Today seminars, and the American Poets Congress. For many decades, she has also been at the forefront of creating educational communities, and has focused on the necessity of archival practices to ensure the memory of some of the twentieth and twenty-first centuries' most precious literary histories and oral recordings. She was one of the founders of the Poetry Project at St. Mark's Church-in-the-Bowery and its director for a number of years, going on to found and direct the Jack Kerouac School of Disembodied Poetics at Naropa University with Allen Ginsberg and Diane di Prima in 1974. She has continued to work at Naropa as Distinguished Professor of Poetics and Artistic Director of its Summer Writing Program. She is the editor of *The Beat Book: Writings from the Beat Generation* and coeditor of *Civil Disobediences: Poetics and Politics in Action, Beats at Naropa*, and *Cross Worlds: Transcultural Poetics*. She is a recipient of the Shelley Memorial Award and a Guggenheim fellowship, and is a chancellor emeritus of the Academy of American Poets. In 2017, Waldman was the keynote speaker at the Jaipur Literature Festival in India, the curator of the Poesía en Voz Alta Festival at Casa del Lago in Mexico City, and she received the prestigious Houtian Prize from China. She has collaborated with a number of artists, performers, and dancers, including Judith Malina of The Living Theatre, choreographer Douglas Dunn, painters Pat Steir and Richard Tuttle, and performance artist and singer Meredith Monk. She regularly performs with her musician family: Ambrose Bye and Devin Brahja Waldman. She makes her homes in New York City and Boulder, Colorado, and reads, performs, and lectures all over the world. Her website is www.annewaldman.org.

JOHN ASHBERY
Selected Poems
Self-Portrait in a Convex Mirror

PAUL BEATTY
Joker, Joker, Deuce

JOSHUA BENNETT
The Sobbing School

TED BERRIGAN
The Sonnets

LAUREN BERRY
The Lifting Dress

PHILIP BOOTH
Lifelines: Selected Poems 1950–1999

JULIANNE BUCHSBAUM
The Apothecary's Heir

JIM CARROLL
Fear of Dreaming: The Selected Poems
Living at the Movies
Void of Course

ALISON HAWTHORNE DEMING
Genius Loci
Rope
Stairway to Heaven

CARL DENNIS
Another Reason
Callings
New and Selected Poems 1974–2004
Night School
Practical Gods
Ranking the Wishes
Unknown Friends

DIANE DI PRIMA
Loba

STUART DISCHELL
Dig Safe

STEPHEN DOBYNS
Velocities: New and Selected Poems: 1966–1992

EDWARD DORN
Way More West

ROGER FANNING
The Middle Ages

ADAM FOULDS
The Broken Word

CARRIE FOUNTAIN
Burn Lake
Instant Winner

AMY GERSTLER
Crown of Weeds
Dearest Creature
Ghost Girl
Medicine
Nerve Storm
Scattered at Sea

EUGENE GLORIA
Drivers at the Short-Time Motel
Hoodlum Birds
My Favorite Warlord

DEBORA GREGER
By Herself
Desert Fathers, Uranium Daughters
God
In Darwin's Room

Men, Women, and Ghosts
Western Art

TERRANCE HAYES
Hip Logic
How to Be Drawn
Lighthead
Wind in a Box

NATHAN HOKS
The Narrow Circle

ROBERT HUNTER
Sentinel and Other Poems

MARY KARR
Viper Rum

JACK KEROUAC
Book of Blues
Book of Haikus
Book of Sketches

JOANNA KLINK
Circadian
Excerpts from a Secret Prophecy
Raptus

JOANNE KYGER
As Ever: Selected Poems

ANN LAUTERBACH
Hum
If in Time: Selected Poems, 1975–2000
On a Stair
Or to Begin Again
Under the Sign

CORINNE LEE
Plenty

PHILLIS LEVIN
May Day
Mercury
Mr. Memory & Other Poems

PATRICIA LOCKWOOD
Motherland Fatherland Homelandsexuals

WILLIAM LOGAN
Macbeth in Venice
Madame X
Rift of Light
Strange Flesh
The Whispering Gallery

ADRIAN MATEJKA
The Big Smoke
Map to the Stars
Mixology

MICHAEL MCCLURE
Huge Dreams: San Francisco and Beat Poems

ROSE MCLARNEY
Its Day Being Gone

DAVID MELTZER
David's Copy: The Selected Poems of David Meltzer

ROBERT MORGAN
Dark Energy
Terroir

CAROL MUSKE-DUKES
Blue Rose
An Octave Above Thunder

Red Trousseau
Twin Cities

ALICE NOTLEY
Certain Magical Acts
Culture of One
The Descent of Alette
Disobedience
In the Pines
Mysteries of Small Houses

WILLIE PERDOMO
The Essential Hits of Shorty Bon Bon

LIA PURPURA
It Shouldn't Have Been Beautiful

LAWRENCE RAAB
The History of Forgetting
Visible Signs: New and Selected Poems

BARBARA RAS
The Last Skin
One Hidden Stuff

MICHAEL ROBBINS
Alien vs. Predator
The Second Sex

PATTIANN ROGERS
Generations
Holy Heathen Rhapsody
Quickening Fields
Wayfare

SAM SAX
Madness

ROBYN SCHIFF
A Woman of Property

WILLIAM STOBB
Absentia
Nervous Systems

TRYFON TOLIDES
An Almost Pure Empty Walking

SARAH VAP
Viability

ANNE WALDMAN
Gossamurmur
Kill or Cure
Manatee/Humanity
Structure of the World Compared to a Bubble

JAMES WELCH
Riding the Earthboy 40

PHILIP WHALEN
Overtime: Selected Poems

ROBERT WRIGLEY
Anatomy of Melancholy and Other Poems
Beautiful Country
Box
Earthly Meditations: New and Selected Poems
Lives of the Animals
Reign of Snakes

MARK YAKICH
The Importance of Peeling Potatoes in Ukraine
Unrelated Individuals Forming a Group Waiting to Cross